Couples Arguing

Couples Arguing

Guidelines to Effective Communication

Tony Gough

Foreword by Jack Dominian

Darton, Longman and Todd
London

First published in 1987 by
Darton, Longman and Todd Ltd
89 Lillie Road, London SW6 1UD

ISBN 0 232 51754 1

British Library Cataloguing in Publication Data

Gough, Tony
    Couples arguing : guidelines to effective
    communication.
    1. Marriage   2. Interpersonal communication
    I. Title
    306.8'72   HQ728

ISBN 0–232–51754–1

Phototypeset by
Input Typesetting Ltd, London SW19 8DR
Printed and bound in Great Britain by
Anchor Brendon Ltd, Tiptree, Essex

For my wife, Jan

who came when my wings were broken
and helped me to fly again

Acknowledgements

My indebtedness to the many people who have influenced my thinking and practice of psychotherapy will be apparent on almost every page of this book. Some of my reading has become so much part of me that it is now impossible for me to attribute my appreciation directly. Where my memory has not let me down, I have acknowledged my sources in the footnote references. In keeping with the non-technical nature of this book, I have tried to keep these to a minimum. The writings of Eric Berne, Sheldon Kopp, Sam Keen, William Schutz, Fritz Perls, Harry Williams and John Rowan have been major influences in my work.

To the late Dr Frank Lake, and that unforgettable Post-Ordination Conference in Catherington House near Portsmouth where we first met back in 1960, my grateful thanks for opening the door into my own inner world; to my friends and colleagues whom I met and worked with through the Clinical Theology Association, where much of my own personal growth took place, I owe an enormous debt: Alison Hunter, therapist, mentor and friend, for her love and openness and for teaching me to confront myself; also, Shirley Ward, Oliver Horrocks, Ted Kettell, Lois Tait, Jackie and Barney Pritchard. To all my friends who had the temerity to challenge the hypocrisy in my dealings with them and who facilitated new insights and growth within me, not least of whom are those I studied and worked with at the Chicago Theological Seminary – Professor Phil Anderson, Peg Stern, Jane Steinhauser, Ray Banner and the Doctor of Ministry Class of '81, my sincere thanks. To the many others who in seminars, workshops and growth groups did not let me settle for an easy or comfortable relationship with them based on self-deception, but who loved me enough to enable me to become honest with both my Self and with them; to the hundreds of couples whom I have counselled over the past thirty years and from whom I have learned so much – to all of you, my grateful thanks.

Contents

Foreword

Marriage is the basis of family life and it is to be found throughout the world. Although polygamy and polyandry exist, the fundamental feature of marriage is the exclusive man-woman relationship. This varies in different parts of the world depending largely on the status of women. When their position is subordinate to and dependent on men, the latter are in charge of the relationship and they do not need to pay much heed to the feelings of their wives. In Western society women's emancipation has made great strides and here marriage is based on a much greater equality of status between the sexes.

This equity between husbands and wives has great advantages and is in keeping with the Christian view that both men and women were created in the image of God and both have a similar dignity of worth. This equality places an enormous emphasis on effective communication between spouses. If sheer social and physical force is no longer the basis of winning an argument, what is left is the honest and persuasive exchange of feelings. These feelings encompass two basic human characteristics, namely affection and anger. Both need adequate expression in order that the relationship may survive and prosper.

From the depths of his counselling experience, Dr Tony Gough has chosen to describe in detail the exchanges of conflict and quarrelling. Every couple is subject to this experience and the way it is handled either enhances or diminishes the relationship. The author skilfully and lucidly describes both the sterile and creative patterns of communication. At the heart of successful quarrelling is the ability to discern, in the midst of the battle, the real pain and agony expressed by the partner and thereby learn how to avoid the repetition of the hurt. This central point of the exchange can be lost in numerous ways, transforming the quarrel into a further wound rather than a healing event. This book successfully describes many of the elements of overcoming dissension.

The marital relationship, as every intimate human exchange, depends for its survival on the balance between love and hate. The successful argument reduces the potential for hate and is therefore an essential tool for marital stability. As such this book is to be welcomed as an addition to the expanding literature becoming available to support marriage.

It can be used in a variety of ways. First of all, counsellors will find it of value in their training and work. Secondly, it can be used as the background for a set subject during a marriage preparation course where couples can be helped with an understanding of effective communication. Thirdly, some couples may wish to read it before or after marriage. In fact this book contains fundamental principles about relating which apply to everyone in an intimate relationship and it will be of use to many professionals such as doctors, nurses, social workers, health visitors and priests, who have to counsel people in all sorts of relationships.

I believe this book will become essential reading for those who work in the field of personal relationships and I wish it every success.

JACK DOMINIAN

Introduction

If the biblical accounts of the birth of human society are anything to go by, couples have been arguing since the beginning of time. In the case of Cain and Abel, their disagreements began in jealousy and anger, and ended in fratricide. Before that, their parents Adam and Eve were involved in the avoidance of responsibility and the 'blaming game'. 'The serpent beguiled me, and I ate,' says Eve pathetically. 'The woman whom thou gavest to be with me, she gave me fruit of the tree, and I ate,' says Adam.[1] The biblical accounts of the creation of the world are closely followed by The Fall, a truly inauspicious beginning for the future world of human relatedness. We are all children of Cain.

Although writing about life, Shakespeare could well have been writing about many of the arguments we have in life when he wrote of 'a tale told by an idiot, full of sound and fury, signifying nothing' (*Macbeth*, V.v.17). Such might well be the epitaph upon the graves of some of the attempts at human communication. Whatever the context – politics, religion, trades unions and management down to the mundane domestic scene – many attempts we have made to express ourselves to another person lie in the ruins of misunderstanding and disharmony. Why is this?

To be sure it did not start out that way. We wanted to say something to someone important to us but suddenly it all seemed to go wrong. We find ourselves shouting at each other, wanting to wound and hurt, and getting out of control. When words fail we begin to use veiled threats or even physical violence when feelings get beyond words. Our frustration in not finding the right words to say or in not being heard properly by the other person gets expressed in gestures or, at worst, a wish to annihilate the other. Such bad endings only give fuel for further heated argu-

[1]The references will be found on p. 129.

ments and so the circle of hostility and bad feelings goes round and round 'signifying nothing'.

Traditionally, of course, some families have been brought up on the model of 'Stop arguing, you two!' Understandable from an over-stressed mother or father, this model however does nothing to teach the younger generation how to argue *constructively*. To suppress latent hostility between people merely affords further fuel to the already smouldering embers buried within. Feelings that are expressed openly and honestly are at least within our control, whereas those that get buried tend to get *acted out* in subversive and sneaky ways that we are not always aware of. Basic hurts and grievances in a relationship need ventilation, not suffocation. In the British culture, the unwillingness to argue is often regarded as a virtue. To make the point, there is (or was) a tradition in the Essex village of Little Dunmow going back to AD 1244 whereby a side of bacon (known as a 'flitch') was awarded to a couple who 'will swear that they have not quarrelled nor repented of their marriage within a year and a day after its celebration'.[2]

The 'Dunmow Flitch' syndrome has infected much of our way of relating to each other, regarding peace and calm (often at any price) as a virtue. We have come to believe that 'arguments are bad; agreements are good'. Contrast this piece of medieval nonsense, with a twentieth-century psychiatrist, Dr Jack Dominian, who reaches nearer to the truth when he writes, 'Every couple quarrels. If they did not then the reality of their happiness would be suspect.'[3]

Before we polarise the 'argument *v.* agreement' too much, we need to bear in mind the corollary which Dr Dominian adds to the above quotation:

> There are two warning signals that something serious is present in the relationship. The first is that quarrels begin to escalate, are repetitive and the issues remain unresolved. The second is the gradual or abrupt cessation of quarrelling with the issues remaining unresolved. In both instances one or more important issues remain unresolved and it is bound to emerge in some further form, possibly in the breakup of the marriage.[4]

The 'Dunmow Flitch Syndrome', therefore, epitomises the dangers in a relationship where issues are never raised and dealt with, but remain hidden beneath an uneasy truce.

The cost of much of this pseudo-peace can be found in the pain, humiliation and hopelessness in many relationships today. Given the unhealthy model of 'no arguing please, we're British!' we find the results in increasing tension and stress. When we can no longer cope, we go to the doctor and share the symptoms which this stress produces in our bodies. The cost to the National Health Service for tranquillisers alone runs into billions of pounds each year. If we don't learn how to complain appropriately, our bodies will. Psychosomatic illnesses are now recognised as originating in some inner conflict. In spite of tranquillisers, there is no pill for human unhappiness. The model of regarding arguing in a bad light is not only out-dated but unhealthy. We cannot afford to go on with the game of 'let's pretend' in our human relationships. The frightening divorce statistics each year (175,000 in England and Wales, 1985) should convince us, if our own experience does not.

The 'stop arguing' model is, however, rooted in a deeper and more powerful belief which is expressed in various ways but essentially it says, 'Don't upset anyone!' This is the cardinal sin. Many people hold passionately to the belief that this is the Golden Rule of life, breaches of which place the perpetrators beyond the pale. There seems to be an unquestioned assumption that other people have a divine right not to be upset. Should we ever upset someone else we will be accused and condemned. 'Now look what you've done; you've upset your mother,' will be accompanied by a withering look intended to bring about a guilty conscience. However, the result of not upsetting anyone has another side.

I remember once counselling a young man whose depression was precipitated by the walking out of his girl-friend. They had lived together for about four years apparently quite happily. One day he arrived home to find her packing her bags. She was leaving, and he naturally asked for an explanation. She told him that she had been having an affair with another man for about six months, and was now leaving to live with him. Distraught, the young man asked her why she had not told him of this relationship before. The answer was, 'I didn't want to upset you'! News of the affair when it first started would indeed have upset the young man for he was devoted to her. But now he was more than upset; he was quite devastated. Her Golden Rule of not upsetting him did not allow time for any discussion about why the new relationship was important and if it was based on any shortcoming in my client's side of the relationship. He was now totally disarmed and felt deeply betrayed. He for one did not appreciate the Golden Rule of 'Never upset thy neighbour', for in the end it was nothing short of deliberate deceit and thinly disguised self-protection on her part. He became suicidal and hence ended up in therapy. Clearly, this couple did not have the opportunity of arguing creatively about the matter when, regardless of the outcome, both people would have had a chance of ventilating their thoughts and feelings appropriately. Even if the outcome had been the same, and she had left anyway, at least they would not have parted with her being left with feelings of guilt, and with him being left with unexpressed hurt, betrayal and anger.

In truth, people do not have the right not to be upset. In expressing our thoughts and feelings, our resentments and pain, to meaningful others we are in fact opening up to them an important part of our Self. This can be an extremely risky business. We will usually do this with people whom we can trust. Yet honest communication is at the heart of every truly intimate relationship. Even if what we communicate is our hostility and anger, this can be done in the name and for the sake of the relationship.

This might be described as 'fighting *for* the relationship' and reminds us of the creative and constructive side of arguing. Dr Arnon Bentovim, the family therapist who commented on a TV documentary about couples arguing, said: 'Arguments don't have to destroy the other. They can be a healthy way of resolving issues. They can lead on to constructive solutions, or they can perhaps relieve tensions enough to allow for periods of sharing and closeness.'[5]

One of the basic assumptions of this book is that on occasions it is far more profitable to confront problems than persons. In any relationship between two people there are always three realities: the two people themselves *plus* the relationship. There is all the difference in the world between fighting against one another and fighting for the relationship. I once heard Harvey, the lovable husband of TV-cop Mary Beth Lacey (*Cagney and Lacey*) say: 'See here, Mary Beth, one half of this marriage is mine, and I'm going to fight for my half of it'.[6] Here is the essence of 'fighting for' the relationship rather than watch it die slowly due to inertia or fear of upsetting someone. Much of the duplicity, deceit and half-truth in some relationships *needs* upsetting if anything healthy is to become of it. This leads us to a third factor which sometimes goes along with a refusal to argue and the fear of upsetting someone: *protection*.

It is often my experience, when I am listening to one of my married clients pouring out a painful story of their misery in the relationship, to ask them, 'Have you told your husband (or wife) about how you feel?' The response is almost always the same. 'Oh, I daren't!' When invited to explain this reluctance to share their experience of pain in the relationship what often transpires is that they are protecting the other partner from the truth. The perception of the client is very often that such revelations would be too much for their partner to cope with, and I get the image of a pathetically weak character who would fall over if confronted by the misgivings or resentment of their partner. On further inquiry, however, the opposite is usually found to be true. The person who is being protected often turns out to be the stronger of the two, calling all the shots, making all the demands, and generally much more capable than the client. My next inquiry is therefore something like this: 'Your partner does not sound as if they need your protection!' Of course, protection can work both ways. The client is often found, after further disclosure, to be protecting *himself or herself*. They lack the words or the ability to say what they would like to convey.[7]

A fourth factor, which contributes to so many of our human interactions proving fruitless and frustrating, concerns our human defence mechanisms.

From childhood, we are in a continuous state of reacting to what is happening around us. Key figures loom large in this process: parents, grandparents, brothers, sisters, aunts and uncles. Two realities come into conflict during this process: our need to assert and express ourselves, and our need to survive.[8] Given a choice, our survival needs will always win. We soon learn what earns parental approval or disapproval. We begin to put two and two together regarding cause and effect. At this childhood stage of our development, our position is essentially that of weakness and vulnerability. Physically and economically, grown-ups have more power than we do; they tell us what to do, or else. Thus the process of *conditioning* gets under way, by which we often have to conform to the needs, wishes or demands of other (grown-up) people. Given the almost god-like status that parents have, especially in our earliest and most formative years, when they are all-knowing and all-providing, their words or actions are rarely

challenged or questioned. Our own perceptions, needs and awareness, along with our emotional world of feelings, are often subju-
gated to those of our parents or older siblings. Since survival is
paramount, we have to find ways of *defending against* much of the
psychic pain and trauma we experience.

It is these acquired 'defence mechanisms', originating in childhood, that are often at the heart of our barren and fruitless
arguments later in life. What are some of these defensive
stratagems?

☐ **Avoidance**: In order to keep the peace at home when young,
we perhaps learnt the art of avoiding any form of confrontation.
Since mother's (or father's) word was law, we soon learned to
conform to her (or his) wishes, avoiding touchy subjects, or
expressing ourselves and our opinions if this would lead to the
wrath of either parent. Submission, appeasement, saying yes (when
we felt 'no'), saying, 'I don't mind' (when we really did mind),
agreeing (when we did not agree) – these and other ways are
instances of avoidance, in order to 'keep the peace'. They helped
us to survive; that is why they still might run very deep within us.
They rescued us in the past. Why give them up now? Like old
faithful friends, we cling to them and they cling to us.

☐ **Denial**: This defence works by denying our real feelings and
needs. Any experience which may threaten our survival, like being
aggressive towards our parents, tends to get buried and
subsequently denied as true of us. Since we are not allowed to
get angry with our parents, we learn to disassociate ourselves from
this emotion and then to deny that we ever get angry with them.
The seriousness of this defensive behaviour is obvious. We are
undergoing a process of detaching part of ourselves from our true
Self (because unacceptable to our parents) and thus growing into
a less than whole person. The long-term result of denying our
true feelings is a total misconception of who we are. 'Me angry?
I never get angry!' As we shall see, this chronic denial of our
true feelings plays havoc in arguments, since those (appropriate)
feelings will tend to be expressed in deviant rather than direct
ways.

☐ **Projection**: This form of defensive behaviour works by taking
the less acceptable parts of our Self, the bits we don't like to think
are really true of us, and accusing others of those feelings or
attitudes. A person with a low estimate of themselves will often
say to others, 'You don't think much of me, do you?', when what

they really mean is, '*I* don't think much of myself'! Projection in arguments between couples is perhaps the most frequent form of behaviour which can spoil or destroy the relationship. When we cannot think well of ourselves, we rarely allow others to do so. Perpetual refusal to accept ourselves as we are will usually result in a refusal to allow anyone else to accept us. I remember vividly a guest arriving at a party I attended who greeted the hostess with a charming compliment on her appearance. It was utterly genuine. The icy reply he received was, 'You probably need new glasses!' I shall never forget the look of pain and hurt on his face, and he later confided in me, 'I shall never pay that woman a compliment again'. Refusing to think well of herself, she was determined not to allow anyone else to think well of her. She was projecting on to him her own negative value of herself. We shall see many examples of this kind of defensive behaviour in the illustrations later in the book.

☐ **Withdrawal**: This can be either physically or emotionally experienced. Physical withdrawal is actually part of an alternative in the psychological 'flight-fight' syndrome. Unable or unwilling to 'fight', the person withdraws from the encounter. They go to bed, for a walk, or in the time-honoured fashion, they go home to mother! This is a refusal to argue and is the source of much frustration in relationships. Emotional withdrawal is when we hide ourselves in our inner castles and simply can't or won't be drawn into an argument. It is a kind of 'make-believe-it-isn't-happening' syndrome. Others can experience this as being 'frozen out', 'cut off', 'ignored' and 'punished'. In spite of its apparent passivity, this behaviour is highly aggressive. It is a non-verbal way of getting our own back. When we speak of children being 'withdrawn' there is usually some deep emotional damage done to the child, and their survival techniques have come to their rescue in order to cut them off from the memory of the painful experience. It is a way of dealing with pain at *an early and totally vulnerable age*. Unfortunately, many people get stuck in this stage of their development, and carry into adulthood *totally inappropriate* means of defending themselves, which in adults are rightly described as 'childish'. We shall see in later chapters[9] how this kind of obsolete behaviour gets in the way of constructive communication.

☐ **Repression**: Some of our most painful experiences in childhood are so threatening, so filled with terror and dread, that by an active mental process such experiences are split-off or detached from our conscious awareness and forcibly not remembered. How these repressed memories show themselves in personal relationships, however, is not hard to discover. A bit of ourselves (the bit we have repressed, since that was the only way we had of defending ourselves against its terror) gets buried *alive*. We may have forgotten it, but it has not forgotten us. The repressed memory acts like a 'ghost', always lurking in the background. If the subject of the repression is, say, some infantile experience of sexual abuse, this may find expression in the difficulty or even impossibility of later adult intimate relationships. The repression will usually have some kind of rationalisation, such as 'I don't like that sort of thing'. The ability to express ourselves as sexual beings is thus hampered. Arguing about this might establish sex as a problem, when the frustration is running high, but material which is so deeply repressed usually needs specialist psychotherapy to eradicate.

These important ways in which we defend ourselves in relationships do have a history behind them. The real problem with them is that, unchallenged and kept out of awareness, they come with us into adulthood where they are usually entirely *obsolete*, like some kind of mental Hadrian's Wall. Erected at a time of intense attack or threat, when we were young, defenceless and vulnerable, and in order to survive, they were absolutely appropriate. Now, in adulthood, they are absolutely *in*appropriate, and instead of defending us they act as a kind of enemy 'fifth column' within, shutting us off from the full enjoyment of life.

The 'couples' in the title assume some importance that is attached to the relationship. It is not restricted to *married* couples or even heterosexual couples. The principles of constructive communication have wide application across the field of human relationships: husband-wife; father-child; mother-daughter; lover-lover. As Dr Jack Dominian has said, 'Communication is a matter of conveying inner needs to each other and reassessing the mutual understanding of each other'.[10]

All the examples in Part II of this book of couples arguing are in fact between men and women. However, the principles of constructive communication in Part I are relevant to every context of life and can improve the quality of the way in which we relate to other people.

It is in the belief that we can unlearn much of our past conditioning which hinders our self-expression and learn new ways of putting what we feel and mean into words that this book is written. I hope it may prove to be a useful kind of relational Highway Code through the journey of life.

Part One
GUIDELINES TO EFFECTIVE COMMUNICATION

There is all the difference in the world between fighting fairly and fighting dirty. We know this from the Marquess of Queensberry rules of boxing where certain blows are considered 'below the belt'. Each of the guidelines that follow contains an exposure of how widespread 'dirty fighting' can be, as well as how to be more constructive in our self-expression. The guidelines are not meant to be memorised like the Ten Commandments, but put into practice in our own personal relationships. In place of the don't-argue, don't-upset-anyone 'protection games' and defensive patterns of behaviour, I shall suggest alternative ways of conveying our meanings and feelings to our significant others. Since we cannot fight today's (adult) battles with yesterday's (childish) weapons, we need a new kind of armoury. If we are to *fight for* improvements in our relationships and the quality of human happiness, we need to find out where we are going wrong and how to put it right.

Hopefully, as we gradually *un*learn the past unhelpful or destructive ways of human relatedness, and adopt more appropriate ways, we can move into the future with a quality of relationships which is based on today's truth, not yesterday's fears.

Summary of the Guidelines

G1. Use direct, rather than indirect, expressions of what you mean to say.

G2. Try making the statements which lie behind your questions.

G3. Own and express your feelings, not just your thoughts.

G4. Respond to the feelings in the statements of the other person.

G5. Affirm the other person when you consider them to be right in their assessment of you.

G6. Don't cloak your own desires or wishes in the usual 'we' or 'one'; try using 'I' instead.

G7. Keep to the main issue at hand; don't get side-tracked into ransacking the 'ancestral cupboard'.

G8. Let your argument stand on its own merits, without dragging in the opinions of others.

G9. Express your needs openly and clearly to the other person.

G10. Whichever partner 'wins', the relationship will probably lose. Confront the real problem rather than one another.

G11. You are not responsible for anyone else's feelings but your own – really!

G12. Take responsibility for what you allow the other person to do to you.

G13. Be specific; avoid generalisations.

G14. Don't project your feelings and ideas on to other people.

G15. Don't stereotype your partner by using depersonalising labels.

G16. Be aware of how you feel inside yourself before, during and after heated arguments; share these feelings with your partner.

G1. USE DIRECT, RATHER THAN INDIRECT, EXPRESSIONS OF WHAT YOU MEAN TO SAY.

The use of indirect communication places a heavy burden on the hearer. S/he has to learn to translate nearly everything that is said. It is like couples communicating in a foreign language. Indirect forms of communication can be either verbal or non-verbal.

Verbal

Take, for instance, this classic piece of verbal nonsense from an episode of *Yes, Minister*. The usually omnicompetent Sir Humphrey Appleby has, for once, been found guilty of gross mismanagement and decides to own up to his Minister:

> The identity of this official whose alleged responsibility for this hypothetical oversight has been the subject of recent speculation is not shrouded in quite such impenetrable obscurity as certain previous disclosures may have led you to assume, and, in fact, not to put too fine a point on it, the individual in question was, it may surprise you to learn, the one to whom your present interlocutor is in the habit of identifying by means of the perpendicular pronoun.[11]

Sir Humphrey means, 'It was I'! But he is not the only one who bombards his hearers with verbiage. We each have our own way of *concealing our meaning*, preferring rather to go round the block once or twice before we come to the point. Of course, past experience might have taught us *not* to be too direct in our communication, or we might not have dared do so for fear of rejection or refusal.

Some people react to the suggestion of being more direct in their communication with others in similar fashion to being asked to take their clothes off in public! Both activities have at least something in common: *exposure*. Being direct means not hiding behind hints, innuendoes and suggestions. 'May I venture to suggest . . .' may sound polite, but it does sound like going round the bush when a simpler, 'I think' would be clearer and more adequate. Of course, we cannot guarantee that others will either appreciate or agree with what we think, but at least they will know what they disagree with.

Four common means of disguising what we want to say are: HINTING, DEFLECTING, WISHING, and SARCASM.

☐ HINTING: Hints are ways of *covering up* what we mean to say. They include just enough exposure to enable the other person to 'take the hint'. Fearful of expressing our needs in a direct way, we 'drop hints' as a safe way of getting the other person to meet our needs.

Example G1.1
HER: I see the Jones' have a new car. But then he earns so much more than you.

HIM: !

This way of hinting could be saying, 'I'd like us to have a new car,' or, 'Why don't you get yourself a decent job with more money'. We know instinctively that she is saying *something*, but by dropping hints she is covering up what she means. Should he respond by, 'You're always wanting something new; you're never satisfied,' she could deny saying such a thing (which she did not, directly) and then blame him for always thinking the worst of her.

☐ DEFLECTING: This means turning away from a direct answer and inviting the opinions of the other person *instead*. It is a way of avoiding the expression of an opinion, which we might have to defend.

> *Example G1.2*
> HUSBAND: Do you like my new shirt?
> WIFE: Some people would say it shouts a bit!

Avoiding her own direct reaction to the shirt, this wife employs the tactic of dragging in 'other people' behind which to shelter her own dislike. Further illustrations of this kind of behaviour will be seen in G8.

> *Example G1.3*
> WIFE: I'm thinking of inviting mother over for lunch on
> Sunday.
> HUSBAND: Now, dear, you know you always get a headache
> when your mother comes!

By turning the effect of mother's visit back on to his wife, the husband does not have to say what effect mother-in-law has on *him*.

☐ WISHING: Many statements beginning with 'I wish' can cover up what we mean to say. For instance:

> *Example G1.4*
> SHE: I wish we could go away for a holiday,
> could mean any of the following:
> 'I am on the point of a nervous collapse',
> or 'You never take me anywhere',
> or 'You're spending so much money on booze that we have no
> money for holidays',
> or 'You never seem to notice how tired I look'.

Her 'wish' can mean almost anything (see further, G9).

☐ SARCASM: This is a veiled form of anger, and unchecked, can poison relationships. The recipient of sarcastic comments usually feels put down or diminished in some way, especially if the comment is expressed in public. This is not surprising when you consider the meaning of the word. The original Greek word means, 'to tear flesh', hence, 'a sharp, bitter or cutting expression or remark' (*Oxford English Dictionary*). Covering up our true feelings, we use sarcasm as a way of expressing them. Sarcasm is designed to wound the other person without ever showing them our knife.

> *Example G1.5*
> SHE: (*arriving half-an-hour late* . . .)
> HE: Punctual, as usual!

His obvious frustration at being kept waiting, which does not need concealing or defending, gets expressed instead behind a sarcastic remark.

Or, take this more humorous example from an episode of the TV comedy, *Only Fools and Horses*:

> *Example G1.6*
> DEL: (*to sour-faced girl at the supermarket check-out counter*) Get your money back, did you?
> GIRL: Where from?
> DEL: The Charm School!

The viewers, of course, dissolve into laughter; but the look on the girl's face tells another story.

What is the importance attaching to these indirect means of communication? *They hide true feelings and meanings of which the speakers may either be aware or unaware.* When they are *unaware* they nevertheless form part of our way of relating to people. When we deliberately suppress our true feelings and meanings, we prevent any deeper issues from surfacing where they might be capable of resolution. When employed as *permanent* habits, indirect or oblique forms of communication can have many harmful results. They ensure that the real feelings attached to unresolved issues *never* get expressed or resolved.

Take Example G1.5. Is there a long-term issue behind this sarcastic comment? Why isn't he confronting her consistent behaviour which he clearly feels strongly about? 'I really resent your being late like this' is at least nearer to the truth. He then feels he has expressed his true feelings instead of veiling them in biting comments. Has he ever considered the effect upon her of his habitual cutting remarks? Does he consider these effects more helpful than an honest confrontation? She may well appreciate a direct and honest confrontation of her habitual lateness so that they can both look at this problem which clearly affects their relationship (see further G.10).

Non-verbal

So far we have looked at some of the ways we communicate indirectly, using words. What about the way we communicate to each other without using words? After all, as the saying goes, 'Actions speak louder than words.'

Perhaps of all the body-language presented to us by others, the eyes can be the most powerful. 'If looks could kill!' is just one of such powerful means of 'saying things' to others.

Now, some of the looks that others can give us are merely of passing interest. If I step on your foot along the road and you give me 'a filthy look', I can tolerate this. It is quite appropriate that you should convey your pain or your expression of my clumsiness in that way. It makes no difference to me; I intend no long-term personal acquaintance with you, anyway. Yet, as a habitual way of expressing feelings and meanings within a deep and lasting relationship, the result of indirect communication can be lethal. 'Deadly looks' need verbalising so that the one giving such looks can be aware of what is going on inside them and learn to accept those feelings as part of themselves. The recipient, also, needs to have an accurate way of interpreting such looks so that he or she can make an appropriate response based on reality, rather than on imagination or fantasy.

Tapping fingers or feet, tight fists, frowns, the tossing of the head or turning of the back to the other person – all these are examples of non-verbal expressions. They all convey meaning, and that meaning needs to be made explicit so that appropriate expression can be made and a resolution found. The body language in connection with our feelings is legendary. For example, the 'cold shoulder' is a way of ignoring or rejecting another person. By confronting these non-verbal expressions, we can ask what they mean. The recipient of such expressions can respond with, 'I am aware that you have not looked at me for the past hour (day, week, whatever) and I would like to know what that means.' Or, 'Your eyes appear to have hatred in them; is that so?' The process of *checking out* is a constructive way of gaining a more honest and direct expression of what the other person is feeling. It is all too easy to imagine what body-language is saying to you; the reality may be quite the opposite. But we do not have to play 'guessing-games' with people who are important to us. We can ask them directly. To the tapping feet or fingers, we might for instance try, 'You appear to be on edge. Is anything the matter?' The word 'appear' is a way of owning what you are experiencing, and leaves room for the other person to correct your interpretation. At least, the inquiry in checking out leads to a mutually shared recognition of what is going on between you. It helps to clear the atmosphere, and then you can both breathe more easily.

G2. TRY MAKING THE STATEMENTS WHICH LIE BEHIND YOUR QUESTIONS.

Although this is linked with G1, there are some particular characteristics which need separate attention. It is true that very often we couch feelings in the form of questions. To this extent, such questions are always *one stage removed* from the truth. Constructive communication is based on the belief that openness and honesty can be sustained only by avoiding such defensive or cryptic statements.

> *Example G2.1*
> HE: (*coming home very late . . .*)
> SHE: And what time do you call this?

It would not actually help her at all to know the precise time, since that is not what she is bothered about. More to the point, perhaps, she could mean:

'I have been worried stiff',
or 'I am angry with you',
or 'I resent your not calling me to say you'd be late'.

In these responses to his lateness, she is conveying her true feelings: anxiety, anger and resentment. He now has the opportunity of responding to her feelings, rather than to her sarcastic question.

At least they both know the issue: she thinks he is late and conveys appropriate emotions. Or, again, consider some of the questions we ask, beginning with the word 'why'.

> *Example G2.2*
> HUSBAND: Why don't you ever cook anything decent?
> WIFE: !

'Why' questions assume the need for information, for reasons, for explanations. All these, on occasions, might be extremely appropriate and useful. The husband's question here, however, does not appear to need a reply. *He is actually making a statement.* But what is he saying? There seems to be some feeling within it, but which feeling? It could range from being a bit tetchy to being thoroughly exasperated. We (and his wife) are left in doubt whether he is referring to her cooking ability (with emphasis on the word 'cook') or whether he is referring to her choice of menu (with emphasis on 'anything'). From his question alone we are left in doubt. What might *the statement behind this question* look like?

Is it – 'I am fed up with my dinner being overcooked',
or   'I am tired of your choice of menu',
or   'This food is inedible'?

Or, might it be –
   'I never receive anything good from you',
or 'My needs never seem to be met',
or 'I feel that I don't matter to you anymore'?

The last three statements lie deeper than the original question which had to do with food, but there might be a connection. Food, what we *take in* or are offered, that which we must *stomach* or *swallow*, the source of energy or well-being – can be used in a metaphorical way in conversation, as in this diagram:

Physical need	Hunger for food
Emotional need	Hunger for affection

Is this husband using a *question* concerning cooking as a veiled way of referring to a statement about feeling uncared for? Which *hunger* is more urgent?

   His question might in fact be concealing an emotional need beneath the subject of food. Something similar is happening in the next example.

Example G2.3
SHE: Darling, do you like my dress?
HE: ?

Is this an innocent way of asking for his opinion on the latest purchase, or could there be something else behind it? She might mean, 'I feel really good in this new dress', or she could mean, 'I need to know you still find me attractive'. Using the diagram above, a deeper more risky statement might lie behind it:

Intellectual need .... approval of new dress

Emotional need .... to be noticed and to be attractive to him

The statement *behind* her question, then, could look like this:

'I need to know you still find me attractive',
or 'I feel so dull and unattractive'.

So the real need could not be met by her husband answering her original question, unless she wanted to read more into his answer than it warranted. Once, however, she reveals the real need (reassurance) he can then respond to it.

Consider this sample list of questions, and some suggested statements which might lie behind them:

Questions (concealing a need)	Statements (expressing a need)
Do you find it hot in here?	I'm too hot in here.
Shall I put the kettle on?	I'd like a cup of tea.
Would you like a meal?	I'm hungry.
Do you love me?	I need to be loved.
Do you really love me?	I'm uncertain about your love.
Must you go on so?	I'm bored.
Do you feel like making love?	I'm feeling sexy.
Was that OK for you?	I need to know you're satisfied.
Does anyone feel cold in here?	I need more heat.

Many of these and other examples reveal once again a conditioned way of obscuring our real needs, and wrapping them up in pseudo-questions. We shall return to this theme in G9. Just by answering the question we often leave the real need unmet. Unmet needs can produce a formidable arsenal from which to assail our partners.

G3. OWN AND EXPRESS YOUR FEELINGS, NOT JUST YOUR THOUGHTS.

If our honest and appropriate feelings were never allowed expression in our childhood, it is likely that we have grown up both highly suspicious of our feelings and with well-worn habits of covering or bottling them up. One particular way we do this is by converting feelings into thoughts. The point is that we don't realise what we are doing until we are made aware of it.

I recall a female client coming to see me who illustrates this particular way of behaving. She was in her late twenties, a professional woman, smartly dressed and very attractive. It transpired that two weeks before she was due to marry, her fiancé rang her up to tell her he could not go through with the marriage. As far as I can remember, our conversation went something like this:

TG: How did you feel when you put the 'phone down?

HER: I thought he must have real doubts about whether it was right to marry me.

TG: But how did you feel?

HER: I thought how important it was not to put any pressure on him, just allow him more time.

TG: That sounds sensible, but how did you *feel?*

HER: My parents were awfully good about it all, and never once criticised him.

TG: And how did *you* feel?

HER: I thought I must let everyone know the wedding had been postponed. Guests were coming from all over ...

TG: I'm sure that was necessary, but how did you feel about his postponing your wedding?

HER: I thought if I started to pressurise him he would back off for good.

TG: Margaret, are you aware that I have asked you five times about your feelings, and each time you told me what you were *thinking?*

This question was met with silence. My own awareness was that it did not seem credible or appropriate that anyone would react to such news with the apparent calm, equanimity and sweet reasonableness that my client was showing. It was all *too* cool and unreal. Her responses appeared to me quite incongruent, given the amount of shock that her story might have suggested. At a later session, I asked for them both to be present. Once again, I tried to help the woman connect up with the true feelings about what he had done, and which my instinct told me she was busy trying to deny or avoid.

TG: I would like you to tell John exactly what you felt about what he had done, once you realised the implications of it all.

HER: (*pausing, her face gradually flushing and tears appearing . . .*) I felt utterly humiliated and hurt beyond words (*fighting back the tears*). I felt rejected and angry that you could do this to me. Do you have any idea what you did to me? How dare you treat me this way? I'm furious with you for not having the guts to tell me to my face. And now I feel scared in telling you all this in case it drives you further away from me.

All this came out with a rush and energy like a lid off a boiling saucepan, and no wonder, for she was boiling inside. She was now a long way from her sweet reasonableness of the previous interview, and in touch with her deepest feelings (hurt, humiliation, rejection, anger and fear) which were far more appropriate to the situation. Once again, by expressing her feelings she got closer to the event and thus to her own inner truth. Moreover, her fiancé understood quite clearly her feelings of hurt and anger, and could now respond to them directly.

This illustrates an important element in constructive conflict: we need to own our feelings, instead of disowning, denying or hiding them. My client was doing this very effectively by converting her feelings into thoughts, and attempting to be totally *rational* about them. In order to be *emotional* she had to take a risk by letting others see and hear what she was feeling. When I tell you what I am feeling I am going one stage deeper in our relationship than when I am merely telling you what I am thinking.[12]

There is an important consequence that we need to be aware of when we disown our feelings: we often try to make other people responsible for them instead. We often hear something like this going on between two people:

You make me feel so angry!
You make me feel so useless!
You make me feel like committing suicide!
You make me feel like walking out!

What is happening here? One partner is trying to get the other to accept responsibility for the first partner's feelings. In other words, 'It's all your fault!' Since on the basis of natural justice and the law of averages this is hardly ever true, the recipient of such blanket statements will retaliate and a dirty battle follows: '*My* fault! What about *you*. . . ?' No one is listening to anyone else, words fall on deaf ears, tempers are running high and voices are raised. Such conflict is destructive of human relationships since nothing is resolved and we don't know what to do about it. The heat and the voices might die down, but the issues underneath have never even been raised to a conscious level and thus lie dormant, festering, awaiting the next verbal onslaught (see further on G7.)

In place of the 'you-make-me-feel' statements, there is another, more creative, way of expressing our feelings. By owning whatever we feel as *ours* (not *yours*) we might state alternatively:

I am feeling angry with you . . .
I am feeling quite useless . . .
I feel like committing suicide . . .
I feel like walking out . . .

These statements retain their original strength, but this time they are being accepted by the speaker as their own, and are not attributed to the other partner. This leaves the recipient free to respond to the feelings of the other without feeling themselves accused or criticised. In truth, no one can *make* (i.e. force) anyone else to feel any particular emotion (we're not talking here about physical pain which others might inflict upon us). To make or try to make others responsible for our feelings is a way of disowning them. It is also a way of attributing power to the other person, and of relinquishing our own power at the same time. 'You-make-me-feel' statements enhance your power, and diminish mine. 'I feel' statements restore my sense of responsibility, my dignity and my own power. We are then back in control of our feelings and can choose what to do about them.

G4. RESPOND TO THE FEELINGS IN THE STATEMENTS OF THE OTHER PERSON.

This implies the necessity *to listen* carefully to what the other person is saying. Arguments sometimes turn on matters of *fact*. 'I didn't ...', 'Yes, you did ...', 'No, I didn't ...', 'Oh yes, you did ...', can go on for hours. The pattern seems to be –

Accusation ... denial ... counter-accusation ... counter-denial ... further accusation ...

This clearly gets us nowhere, only hot under the collar. One way of breaking out of what is in fact a destructive pattern of relating, is to focus on what you are aware the other person might be *feeling*. Now, remember, your awareness might be wrong, so go carefully. 'You're angry,' can lead to, 'No, I'm not ...' 'Yes, you are ...' etc. So a tentative response might sound like this:

'You appear to be very angry about that',
or 'I am aware how angry you sound right now.'

If this is received by the other person as accurate, a follow-up statement could be –

'I'd like you to tell me anything else you're angry about ...'

There is usually something constructive about being *heard* at this level of our feelings. It means –

'Your feelings do not frighten me away',
'I can cope with your anger',
'Your feelings are not going to destroy me',
'I can accept your feelings'.

This openness can lead to a more appropriate expression of what we feel, since in a way we are *giving the other person permission* to go ahead and state directly what they feel, and this might be a novel experience for some people. We do not need to be intimidated by the free expression of other people's feelings, or to feel responsible for them. We are then free to respond with our own feelings, like –

'Thank you for expressing your anger at my being late this evening. I had no idea you felt that way. You've always tended to shield me from your anger before. I feel sad that my actions have been the occasion of your pain.'

Awareness of, and respect for, our own feelings leads on to awareness and respect for the feelings of others. This provides us with a more constructive model for dealing with conflict than mere excuses for lateness concerning British Rail, the stopped watch, the forgotten diary or that rush job at the office. All these *may* be true and relevant to *why* we were late; but they are not the most important element in the interaction between the two people. The immediate feelings need expression and acknowledgement; the facts of the matter can come later.

G5. AFFIRM THE OTHER PERSON WHEN YOU CONSIDER THEM TO BE RIGHT IN THEIR ASSESSMENT OF YOU.

This is a method of defusing an argument by accepting any statement others make about us which we know to be true. This process is sometimes known as being able to 'lean into the accusation'.[13] It really means acknowledging the truth of what others say about us.

'You're right; I can be very impatient at times . . .'

sounds honest and straightforward, rather than dismissing such statements and immediately jumping in with a counter-accusation –

'That sounds rich coming from you. . . !'

We naturally want to defend ourselves in arguments, but it is destructive of human relationships to defend what is *not* true of us and which anyone with half an eye can see is false. Yet it is not easy to allow ourselves to acknowledge this falsity. It is a mark of maturity when we can do so. The barrier to such honest acceptance of the truth about ourselves was possibly constructed way back in childhood. Such acknowledgements *then* would have been taken as a sign of weakness, and would be exploited by unfeeling others. It still feels unsafe to acknowledge the shadowy side of our personality, but in a loving relationship it is often essential to do so.

I recall working in a group where a woman was sharing in some depth her sense of horror when a long-term friend of her family sat down next to her after a meal, and out of the blue started to undo the buttons of her blouse! The action was totally unexpected and she was deeply shocked by this uncharacteristic assault. As we listened to this story, our group leader happened to be sitting next to the speaker, but on a higher chair. He pointed out to her and the group that from where he was sitting, much of her bust was exposed to his view. He suggested to the woman the possibility of her giving her family friend a double message. Immediately, the atmosphere in the group was charged with indignation. Two other female group members responded with instant anger to the group leader, and to what they heard as the attribution of responsibility to the *woman* for the assault! (It is, of course, part of the common male mythology that women contribute significantly to sex attacks made upon them. This is not so.) The group leader was surprised by the attack, but eventually he decided to 'lean into the accusation' and declare *his own ambivalence* towards women's breasts which originated in some very painful childhood experiences as a new-born baby. The 'double message' he had projected on to the woman was in fact his own ambivalence. Graciously he accepted this, and the group movingly accepted him and his painful honesty in sharing his story with us. This is human relatedness of a high order. I realise that.

Yet it is attainable when we take the risk of agreeing with others about their accurate perception of our own character and its defects. Since we are then not using up our energy in denying that which we know to be true about ourselves, we can direct that energy into sharing, and receiving the acceptance of the other person.

G6. DON'T CLOAK YOUR OWN DESIRES OR WISHES IN THE USUAL 'WE' OR 'ONE'; TRY USING 'I' INSTEAD.

A time-honoured way of covering up what we really want is to use the all-inclusive word 'we'.

> 'What we all want is . . .'

really boils down to –

> 'What *I* really want is . . .'

For some people, this direct expression of their needs is a risky thing.

The use of the vague 'we' actually hides our own individual desires or needs within a global form. It is essentially a defensive means of communicating, so that if challenged, we can always reply –

'Well, of course, it's not what I want, but I thought it was what *you* wanted.'

'We' statements can be a simple way of sneaking in our own wants by attributing them to other people. It is nearer the truth to make the 'I' statements which lie within this 'we'. This means owning the statement or desire we are about to make. Since the bald use of 'I' is thought in some circles to be uncouth, the euphemistic 'one' was doubtless invented to get round the problem.

'One finds it all very embarrassing',

sounds quaint, even pedantic.[14] The avoidance of the word 'I' is, of course, a device which enables us to evade the *explicit* feelings or ideas we may have. When we feel we are being included in someone else's use of 'we', it is possible for us to disassociate ourselves from the remark: 'You may feel like that, but I certainly don't.'

Individual partners often find themselves getting included in someone else's statements. It then becomes an unchallenged assumption: 'We don't seem to be getting anywhere, do we?' Decoded, this becomes: 'I feel as if I'm getting nowhere.' The other partner can now respond to this feeling without having to expend energy disassociating from the previous all-inclusive 'we', and free from any blame for the state of affairs. 'I' statements are more open to the individual's own inner awarenesses and feelings and thus closer to their own personal truth.

There is another, more subtle, side to the use of 'we'. Unchecked, it can reinforce the idea that couples must think, feel and behave like Siamese twins. Opinions, hobbies, activities, community or political allegiances, have to be shared together and individuality must be sacrificed on the altar of 'togetherness'. This phenomenon is, of course, a form of possession, when some couples work to a 'You belong *to* me' script, instead of one which reads, 'You belong *with* me'. When this is the case, 'we' will be a means to reaffirm such possessiveness.

'We' statements can also be a form of control. When couples come to see me, I often hear one of them telling me, 'We never argue, do we?' It can sound like a threat ('Disagree, and I'll never speak to you again!'). I invariably ask the silent partner if they ever wish they *did* argue, and whether or not they are happy to be included in the 'we' statement. Most of the replies contain a disassociation from the views expressed by their partner and the way is then open for further exploration into forbidden areas of the relationship.

G7. KEEP TO THE MAIN ISSUE AT HAND; DON'T GET SIDE-TRACKED INTO RANSACKING THE 'ANCESTRAL CUPBOARD'.

One of the long-term problems many couples face is that they never actually resolve any of the issues they argue about.[15] Because of their defective methods of arguing, matters simply get left unresolved time and time again. What happens to all that 'unfinished business', the issues which people still feel deeply about but which have not yet been settled between them? Very often, in spite of the bickering and shouting and other ways of trying to hurt the other person, unresolved matters simply get picked off the floor and stacked neatly away in our mental or matrimonial 'ancestral cupboard' where they are primed and ready for discharge at the next verbal battle. As one writer puts it, yesterday's failures are used for today's ammunition.[16] This way, nothing is ever let go of or forgotten. Nothing is ever left behind; everything we said in our last argument will be repeated. How is it that some arguments always seem to end up with 'your mother', or 'your affair last year', or 'and you're no good in bed either!'

Pause for a moment, and recall the themes of the recent arguments you have had with your partner or relative. Do you recognise any pattern to them? Do they always end up with the same accusation or grievance you started with? If this is so, there are things in the ancestral cupboard of your relationship which need urgent attention. The little thing we may start out arguing about might not be the main issue at all. Underneath might lurk an even more important issue which will only come out in the heat of battle. It is important in arguing that you *agree on the agenda*: 'What are we fighting about?'

Let's take the accusation, '. . . and you're no good in bed either!' as an example. Behind this accusation might be a *long-term* problem regarding sexual satisfaction in the relationship. It is an example of 'dirty fighting' to drag this out of the cupboard and hurl at a partner in the context of an argument which began elsewhere. This kind of statement is meant to wound, to humiliate, to crush. Why is the aggrieved partner not bringing this matter up as a separate issue, since there seems to be a lot of energy behind it? Are they afraid to do so? Can they only *allude* to it in the context of a bigger row, since it is only then that it is safe to do so and when any positive resolution is impossible? If there are matters which get thrown up each time couples argue, then there is a need to sit down at a calmer moment and draw up some kind of agenda for discussion in order of priority. Sexual problems often lie at the heart of many disagreements between couples, but are rarely aired.* The pathetic – 'I don't want to hurt his/her feelings' – is simply an evasion caused by embarrassment, and is wrapped up in a false belief that they are protecting the other partner. Using the insights in G6, this statement might be more accurately stated, '. . . and I get no satisfaction in our sex life'. This 'I' statement cannot be refuted. It is an honest *owning up* to one's own dissatisfaction and, by saying it that way, it at least invites, if not actually includes, taking some personal responsibility for that state of affairs, since 'it takes two to tango'.

When there are deep-seated differences within a partnership or marriage, they don't just go away. They fester, and become part of the store-cupboard of resentments and pain which only get expressed when thrown around in a quarrel. The cupboard certainly needs looking at, for there are important issues stored away in there, but it does not really help to throw up the matter of sexual dissatisfaction in the context of a row about money.

There was a healthy model I noticed in an episode of the TV soap *Dallas*. Pam Ewing was in her office in the middle of an argument with someone when the secretary walked in and said she was wanted urgently on the telephone. 'I can't deal with that right now,' she replied, and this might be one way of batting off side issues when a more important issue is at hand. If, in the middle of an argument about housekeeping money, the sexual issue suddenly gets thrown in, then something like Pam Ewing's reply might be a useful one: 'I hear you're not satisfied with our sex life; neither am I come to that. But I don't want to talk about that right now; we're talking about money . . .' Or, 'Now that you've raised the matter of our sex life, I'm quite happy to drop

---

*Surveys suggest that there could be up to 15 million men and women in Britain whose sex lives are causing them misery.

this discussion about housekeeping money if you think our sex life is more important.'

There can be a mutual agreement to change the agenda, dropping one (side) issue in order to discuss a second (main) one. It might be a big leap to go from housekeeping to sex, but think of it this way. Underneath the arguments concerning money (which come out as, 'I'm not satisfied with what you're giving me . . .') *might* be the greater, and perhaps more important, matter of sexual dissatisfaction, when the *identical words* could be used, '(sexually) I'm not satisfied with what you're giving me'. When the real issue is exposed, secondary rows about money can be dropped, and the couple can get down to see how their sex life can be improved. This is a useful way of tracing what is the real issue. Sometimes in arguments, if we dare risk saying it, when either resentments or frustrations are being expressed, it is possible to ask, 'Is there anything else you're angry/resentful/frustrated about?' This invites an honest response, and tells your partner that you are ready to look at more urgent issues. When they get resolved, the cupboard gets emptied of a few past grievances, and makes future arguments that much more relevant to contemporary issues rather than delving back into the past history of the relationship.

Some hurts, of course, can never be forgotten. We sometimes wish they could, but they can't. They run too deep. However, there is the possibility of *forgiveness*. For me, the simplest way of explaining forgiveness is this: *it is the refusal to claim compensation for past injuries or wrongs*. It is like handing back an IOU, to which we have a rightful claim for payment, and refusing to demand a settlement. This is not to deny what happened in the past; rather, it is a voluntary act of relinquishing our rightful claim upon the other person and a refusal to hold that against them any more. That way, the ancestral cupboard gets emptied and we can concentrate our energies on issues which matter in the here and now.

G8. LET YOUR ARGUMENT STAND ON ITS OWN MERITS WITHOUT DRAGGING IN THE OPINIONS OF OTHERS.

Here is another common feature of family rows. In order to strengthen our attack, we call upon reinforcements in the form of other people's opinions.

In an ideal argument, it should be sufficient for the person to state the case against the other partner simply from their own standpoint. It is enough for a husband to say, 'I feel utterly uncared for by you,' without having to add, for example, 'and the kids feel the same way,' or '. . . and your mother says you've always been a cold bitch'. These latter additions might in fact be true, but that is something for others to deal with. The husband's feelings of lack of care from his wife are *sufficient* grounds for this particular confrontation. It is permissible for us to seek to get our own needs met, without appearing to launch out on a crusade on behalf of other people, who are in any case perfectly able to fight their own battles. Perhaps the husband believes that *mere numbers* on his side will change his wife. They rarely do. They merely invite reprisals. Two can play at the 'numbers game', and the argument tends to go round in circles getting nowhere.

To reinforce our argument by quoting other people is to engage in the syndrome we met in G6, that is, making 'we' statements instead of 'I' statements. By narrowing down our case to what 'I' believe or feel, the other person is able to deal with at least a manageable amount of material. This heightens the sense of immediacy between the two people arguing so that it becomes a truly 'I–Thou' encounter. It lessens the chances of being side-tracked to other people's views when the focus of attention goes from 'I–Thou' (in here) to 'Thou–Them' (out there). A healthy response to the 'numbers game', therefore, might sound like –

'I hear what my mother has told you, but I can only deal with what you are feeling right now.'

or 'I'm more interested in what you are feeling right now. Let's leave my mother out of this.'

This keeps to the main issue (G7) concerning the husband's feeling of lack of care.

G9. EXPRESS YOUR NEEDS OPENLY AND CLEARLY TO THE OTHER PERSON.

If there isn't exactly a written taboo in our culture regarding the open expression of our needs, most couples often act as if there is.

I remember that in my own childhood it was often said to me that I must 'wait until you are asked'. The implication was that it was somehow improper or impolite to ask for anything directly. But often I would wait all day to be asked, and never was! When the 'waiting game' is played between couples, let us see what can happen.

Jane needs to see more of John. John works late during the week, plays golf on Saturday ('I must have some recreation'), and is immersed in paper-work all day Sunday ('Must get this in order for Monday'). All this busy-ness, of course, is said to be essential to keep the family wolf from the door. But Jane needs to see more of John. Seeing his work schedule, his tired look when he gets home, ready for dinner, telly and bed, she does not like to confront him with her needs. But Jane needs to see more of John, and ends up in the classic 'double-bind'. A double-bind is the name given to situations in which no matter what you do, you lose. It is the classic loser's script: heads they win, tails I lose. To express *her* needs to John would seem as if she is not only insensitive to *his* needs but actually adding to his worries. So Jane sacrifices her needs to John's and settles for the 'waiting game'. After a while, Jane's needs begin to emerge in a different, more sinister, form. For when we do not express our needs directly (through the 'front door') they have a nasty habit of sneaking off out of the 'back door' (see G1). Instead of *acting* on her real needs, Jane now begins to *react*. In subtle, and of course subconscious, ways Jane begins to get her own back. Important documents are inexplicably mislaid; vital telephone messages are 'forgotten', dinner engagements are sprung on him at the last moment ('Oh, sorry John. Didn't I tell you. . . ?') And – the *coup de grâce* – she is constantly having headaches in bed!

Is there an alternative to this destructive pattern of the 'double-bind' syndrome? I believe there is.

Example G9.1

JANE: Do you realise, darling, that we've hardly spoken to each other this week? You seem so busy lately, but I must tell you that I need to have more of your time. I miss talking and sharing with you.

JOHN: Well you know how busy I've been . . .

JANE: Yes, I know that; but you don't seem to have heard what I said. I need to see more of you, John.

JOHN: Once this contract is out of the way it'll all be different . . .

JANE: You're still not hearing me, John. I need you to respond to my needs.

What is going on here? Jane is keeping John to the point (G7) and showing clearly and sympathetically her awareness of *his* difficulties. She is also trying to get John to respond to *her* need, whereas he does not hear this and responds only with his problems. John is not hearing Jane, hence her persistence.

Of course, merely by expressing your needs, it does not mean that there will be an immediate compliance on the part of the other person. But Jane is placing her need on top of her agenda and letting John know honestly how she feels. Repeated refusal by John to listen may mean that Jane will have to employ other tactics (see G10 and G12).

Open and clear expression of our needs is in stark contrast to the sneaky ways seen in some styles of arguing.

☐ NAGGING is the most familiar way of in-fighting. No one likes it, except the inveterate nagger for whom it has become a way of life, an unconscious way of relating to people. Eric Berne, in his book *Games People Play*, refers to the game called 'Ain't it Awful?'[17] and this is the nagger's paradise, which can go on for ever. Nagging is like a continuous downpour of acid rain on a relationship, stripping it of its beauty and splendour. Often the subject of the nag-nag-nag syndrome is lost sight of, and degenerates into a more *generalised hostility* towards the other person. Antagonism becomes a kind of poisonous atmosphere in the home, a living and breathing hell. Nagging might have begun with a need expressed directly but which was not heard or responded to by the other person, and after a while the real need gets pushed into the background where it joins up with all the other unmet needs of this person, adding to the cacophony of generalised complaints which are 'all the fault' of the other person.

☐ MANIPULATING is another way of getting the other person to respond to our needs. As the word suggests, there is a lot of 'string-pulling' involved in this activity. It is a way of getting our needs met in an underhanded manner, by actually contriving to give the other person no alternative but to do things our way. Whenever you find yourself constantly giving way in a relationship, the chances are that manipulation is at work somewhere.

☐ THREATENING is a more obvious form of manipulation. Needs are not so much revealed as taken for granted. 'Things will be done my way – or else!' It is a blatant use of force. Threats of leaving, of suicide (violence to oneself) or physical attack (violence to others) are, for some couples, part of their staple diet.

> *Example G9.2*
> 'If you see that other woman again, I'm going to kill myself, and the children!'
> 'If you see that man again, I'll smash your face in!'

☐ INTIMIDATING is a slightly softer form of threatening. At the heart of this word lies the key to its significance: *timid*. It means to render timid or to make afraid. Whereas in threatening the means used suggests 'I'm *stronger* than you', in intimidation the opposite is assumed, 'You're *weaker* than me'. Many couples are governed by the way in which one of the partners gains and retains the upper hand by this means of coercion.

As we saw in Example G9.1. Jane does not have to resort to any of these damaging means in order to express her needs to John. She does so clearly and openly without any suggestion of sanctions. John, when he finally hears Jane, can respond to her needs without feeling cornered and by using his freedom of choice.

G10. WHICHEVER PARTNER 'WINS' IN AN ARGUMENT, THE RELATIONSHIP WILL PROBABLY LOSE. CONFRONT THE REAL PROBLEM RATHER THAN ONE ANOTHER.

Most arguments between couples are based on the 'winners-and-losers' model. It is the model taken from the world of competitiveness: as in boxing, someone must be seen to win and the other must be seen to either concede (by throwing in the towel!) or be knocked out. This pugilistic model is harmful for a number of reasons.

☐ FIRST, the model has an in-built assumption that the other person is the 'enemy' who must be 'beaten'. It's a case of 'you *or* me'. This polarises the couple into the one in the 'blue corner' and the one in the 'red corner'. They are on opposite sides, out to get each other. It is warfare, in which any weapons will do. They want to win at any price, and any talk of 'fighting fair' will be dismissed as a sign of contemptuous weakness. Chances are, they wouldn't have got this far into the present book! The whole relationship is based not on enjoyment, but on survival, and for that they must fight by fair means or foul.

The most classic example of this kind of vicious verbal warfare that I have come across is in Edward Albee's play, *Who's Afraid of Virginia Woolf?* which later became a classic movie with Richard Burton and Elizabeth Taylor in the leading roles of George and Martha. The dialogue is white-hot in its intensity, and searing in its effects. They claw and bite and kick one another verbally. No insult is tempered, no vulnerability spared, no weak spot left unexploited. For example:

GEORGE: Actually, I'm rather worried about you. About your mind.

MARTHA: Don't you worry about my mind, sweetheart!

GEORGE: I think I'll have you committed.

MARTHA: You what?

GEORGE: I think I'll have you committed.

MARTHA: Oh, baby, aren't you something!

GEORGE: I've got to find some way to really get at you.

MARTHA: You've got at me, George . . . you don't have to do anything. Twenty-three years of you has been quite enough.

GEORGE: Will you go quietly, then?

MARTHA: You know what's happened, George? You want to know what's really happened? It's snapped, finally. Not me . . . it. The whole arrangement. You can go along . . . forever, and everything's . . . manageable. You make all sorts of excuses to yourself . . . you know . . . this is life . . . the hell with it . . . maybe tomorrow he'll be dead . . . maybe tomorrow you'll be dead . . . all sorts of excuses. But then, one day, one night, something happens . . . and SNAP! It breaks. And you just don't give a damn anymore. I've tried with you, baby . . . really. I've tried.

GEORGE: Come off it, Martha.

MARTHA: I've tried. I've really tried.

GEORGE: You're a monster . . . you are.

MARTHA: I'm loud, and I'm vulgar, and I wear the pants in this house because somebody's got to, but I am not a monster. I am not.

GEORGE: You're a spoiled, self-indulgent, willful, dirty-minded, liquor-ridden . . .

MARTHA: Snap! It went snap. Look, I'm not going to try to get through to you any more . . . I'm not going to try. There was a second back there, maybe, there was a second, just a second, when I could have gotten through to you, when maybe we could have cut through all this crap. But that's past, and now I'm not going to try.

GEORGE: Once a month, Martha! I've gotten used to it . . . once a month and we get misunderstood Martha, the good-hearted girl underneath the barnacles, the little Miss that the touch of kindness'd bring to bloom again. And I've believed it more times that I want to remember, because I don't want to think I'm that much of a sucker.

MARTHA: . . . I'm not going to give a damn what I do, and I'm going to make the damned biggest explosion you ever heard.

GEORGE: You try it and I'll beat you at your own game.

MARTHA: Is that a threat, George? Huh?

GEORGE: That's a threat, Martha.

MARTHA: You're going to get it, baby.

GEORGE: Be careful, Martha . . . I'll rip you to pieces.

MARTHA: You aren't man enough . . . you haven't got the guts.

GEORGE: Total war?

MARTHA: Total.[18]

Well, I mentioned (G7) about ransacking the ancestral cupboard, and in this excerpt we overhear two experts in the art of destructive confrontation. In seeking to 'win', they actually wound the relationship. It is 'total war'.

☐ SECONDLY, given the assumption that the other person is now the 'enemy', this kind of confrontation solves nothing. It is merely a way of indulging in mutual assassination. It leads to the destruction rather than to the enhancement of the relationship. It destroys mutual trust, since intimate secrets shared with a partner suddenly become weapons in a war of humiliation. Such secrets shared in moments of intimacy and enjoyment, are turned into expressions of disgust or vilification. Never again can that partner trust the other with any further self-disclosure, or divulge any more inner fantasies or fears. A part of that person is now blocked off, possibly for good, and so there will be less than a 'whole' relationship. A vital ingredient in all good relationships – trust – is destroyed. The other person might have won the battle in the total humiliation of the other, but the relationship itself has lost part of its essence, its soul.

Dr George Bach, in his book *The Intimate Enemy*,[19] has a helpful antidote to this kind of fighting. As he puts it, 'the only way to win intimate encounters is for both partners to win'. Instead of polarising our model of fighting

ME ←——————————————————→ YOU

a more profitable model would be one in which the energies of both partners are focused upon the *problem*, hence

ME & YOU ——————————————→ PROBLEM

Here I visualise (and at consultations often suggest) the couple changing seats, and instead of sitting face-to-face, eyeball to eyeball, they sit next to each other, facing 'the problem'. This way, the energies of both partners can be directed at the real issue at hand, instead of expending it on attacking one another.

> *Example G*10.1
> HE: What are you aware of?
> SHE: I notice our sex life has been less frequent recently.
> HE: Yes, I've noticed that too.
> SHE: I don't like it that way.
> HE: Neither do I.
> SHE: I'd really like to work towards some improvement in this area. Would you?
> HE: I'm glad you've brought this up, because I was feeling a bit embarrassed to do it myself. Maybe our sex life has been a bit routine, and I have some ideas I'd like to share with you ...

In this example, we see the two people concerned with improving their sex life, facing the problem together rather than confronting one another. They are here pooling their energies, not polarising them; that is, they appear to be pulling together, not pulling apart. In helping the relationship to 'win', they both win. They are fighting the problem of their sex life, not each other.

G11. YOU ARE NOT RESPONSIBLE FOR ANYONE ELSE'S FEELINGS BUT YOUR OWN – REALLY!

Whenever I put this idea to my clients there is usually a common response: astonishment! This is, naturally enough, understandable. As a post-Christian culture we have probably been raised on the idea that the unforgiveable sin is to upset other people. It's a mixture of 'think of other people first'; 'be kind to others', 'don't be selfish', 'never mind how you feel – put other people's feelings before your own'. As a cultural or personal ethic these ideas, on the surface, seem utterly desirable. To argue against them is to vote against motherhood and apple pie!

But there is another, more sinister, side to this seductive ethic. It can produce a false sense of responsibility leading to neurotic guilt feelings, and also an abandonment of a true sense of responsibility. Let's look at these ideas further and see how they work out in practice.

> *Example G11.1*
> Fred is experiencing a great deal of frustration in his
> marriage to Mary. This concerns their very infrequent
> sexual activity. He feels his natural desires and needs are
> not getting met. Yet, each time he starts to approach Mary
> about the subject, she reacts strongly by saying he just wants
> her for one thing, that he is obsessed with sex, and she
> goes to bed with a headache. Mary does not talk to Fred
> for a few days. Fred feels terribly guilty about the effect
> of his disclosure to Mary, and feels responsible for hurting
> her. During the days of silence, he tries to be a model
> husband, doing things to please Mary, and gradually she
> comes round again. Fred feels trapped between not
> wanting to hurt Mary but at the same time wanting to be
> honest with her about how he feels about their sex life.

What is going on here? Is there a hidden agenda?

Whenever Fred mentions sex, Mary punishes him. She makes no response to his expression of feelings and needs, and counter-attacks him for mentioning the subject by 'freezing him out'. Because Fred does not like to see Mary hurt (nor her freezing him out) he tries to please her, by being 'a good little boy', and making up for having hurt her. Fred is, in fact, *taking responsibility for Mary's feelings*, and adjusting his own behaviour in consequence. He is feeling bad about the effect his remarks had on Mary. In other words Mary is saying to Fred, 'You are responsible for hurting me and making me sad and for having a headache. And I'm going to make you pay . . .' By his reaction to what Mary is both acting out and implying, Fred is saying: 'I am feeling sorry for making you sad and for hurting you with my demands, and I will try and make up for it by being good/helpful/compliant.'

What is going on between Mary and Fred is sick, because there is obviously dis/ease here. But how does Fred deal with it in a more constructive way? For there is *another* bit of Fred that is saying something which differs from his first reaction. Maybe something like this: 'Dammit! I feel so frustrated. I just can't win! If I mention my sexual needs, Mary freezes me out for days, and I can't stand that. And if I don't mention them, I go on feeling frustrated and not fulfilled. Either way, I lose.' Fred is in the classic double-bind situation. He has to carry his own pain, and is also taking responsibility for Mary's pain as well.

How would an honest confrontation of Mary sound like, if Fred were to behave differently? Suppose Fred did *not* take responsibility for Mary's feelings, but only his own, what difference would this make? It might sound like this:

> 'Mary, I want to share something with you that is important to me, and I believe to our marriage. You must be as aware as I am that our sex life is now almost non-existent, and I miss making love to you. I am afraid of saying this because each time I do, you seem to punish me by not speaking to me, and I hate that. In the past I have been feeling responsible for your feelings when I raise the matter of sex. I honestly don't want you to feel hurt by what I say, but I must share with you how unhappy I feel. I am feeling desperately unhappy about how things are between us, and matters only seem to be getting worse.
>
> I am willing to take responsibility for the way I feel, and talking to you like this is a hell of a risk, for I don't know what you're going to do with what I am saying. I want to discuss the issue of sex like two adults in the interests of our mutual happiness.'

And, supposing Mary were really to *hear* what Fred is saying, and to respond to him in her adult awareness instead of her usual childishness?

> 'Fred, it's not easy for me to respond to what you've said; I feel embarrassed and guilty, especially when I remember what I have been doing to you in the past. I have been

blaming you for being "obsessed with sex", but I know it's not true. You are a kind and caring man. I see now I've been hurting myself too. The trouble is I need to know you need *me*, not just my body. I want our sex to mean something, and just recently I've not seemed to matter to you. I have needs, too, Fred. I've not always been honest about them and I've kept them from you. Maybe we're just beginning to change all that?'

Mary has now 'come clean' about her needs, and as we saw in G10, Fred and Mary can now, together, confront the problem of intimacy in their marriage, *free from blaming* the other person for how they feel.

This will mean for most of us learning a new kind of vocabulary. Blaming – making others responsible for how we feel – is not constructive. It creates more problems for the couple. Instead, let us see how a *change in communication* would look:

Old style of blaming – making YOU responsible for how I feel	*New style of taking responsibility for how I feel*
You make me feel angry.	I am feeling angry.
You're always blaming me.	I am always feeling blamed.
You don't love me.	I feel unloved.
You're always criticising.	I'm always feeling criticised.
You're hurting me.	I'm feeling hurt.
You never listen.	I never feel heard.

Taking responsibility for our feelings means that we *own them* as ours. By attributing our feelings to other people, we *disown them* and project them on to others. Owning our feelings leaves others free to respond to us more openly, without accusations of blame or criticism. It creates a more neutral atmosphere in which to sort out problems. More importantly, making others responsible for the way we feel is actually attributing *power to others over us*, and at the same time diminishing our own sense of power and control over our own lives. 'You make me feel' statements add to our own sense of worthlessness and weakness. 'I am feeling' statements enhance our sense of self-respect and dignity, and restore to us a sense of control and direction. Taking responsibility for our own feelings, and refusing to take responsibility for others' feelings, is a mark of growth and adulthood. It is also a sign of love, not indifference. It was in the name of love and for the sake of their enjoyment of intimacy that Fred and Mary needed to learn a new way of sharing.

G12. TAKE RESPONSIBILITY FOR WHAT YOU ALLOW THE OTHER PERSON TO DO TO YOU.

This is another way of looking at the subject raised in G11 but deserves fuller examination. One of the most frequently heard complaints in my counselling practice concerns the hardships the client is experiencing at the hands of other people. Long catalogues of wrongs, slights, insults, pain and humiliation are trundled out and recounted at great length. To be sure, most of them make painful hearing. The focus is, of course, on *the other person* and *their* behaviour; what *they* are doing to make the client's world a living hell. Having heard what others are doing to my client, my curiosity then turns to the client him/herself. What part are they playing in this relationship?

One female client came to see me, and unfolded her story. It concerned her marriage which had been going on for over twenty years. A painful saga began to emerge, of her husband's humiliating behaviour, treating her like dirt. Sexual intercourse verged each time on rape, and the husband appeared to be totally indifferent to my client's feelings. There seemed to be no respect or care. She was totally dominated by him. Her last painful words were, 'I feel I'm not a person anymore; I feel just like a set of genitals!' The feelings of self-loathing and disgust, of hopelessness and pain, were obvious. We sat silent for a few minutes, after which I asked her just one question: 'Tell me, why did you allow your husband to treat you like that?' She received that question with a look of growing amazement and bewilderment, as if I'd just hit her over the head with a telephone pole! I could see her struggling inwardly with the import of the question, which of course included an assumption on my part. After a few minutes she stammered, 'You mean, I have a choice?' 'Yes,' I said, 'that's precisely what I mean.' I was by no means unsympathetic to the woman's story, but her *perception* of what was happening was faulty. It was *her behaviour* that needed to change, not the husband's, for he saw no need to change it. *She was not taking responsibility for what she was allowing him to do to her.* My loaded question was intended to bring to her awareness her own power of choice and it had just that effect.

Another, less fraught, story concerned another female client. She was a lady in her fifties, a very keen member of her church who often gave lifts to the older members of her congregation. On one occasion the old lady in question invited my client in for a cup of coffee. 'She kept me there for five hours!' my client said heatedly. I could not resist a humorous response:

TG: Five hours?

HER: Yes, five hours!

TG: How did she do it?

HER: Do what?

TG: Keep you there.

HER: What do you mean (*puzzled*)?

TG: I mean, how did she keep you there all that time? Did she lock the door or chain you to the radiator?

HER: Oh, no. Nothing like that (*giggling*).

TG: You mean, you *could* have left any time?

HER: Yes.

TG: Oh, I see. You mean you allowed yourself to be kept there all that time, but are trying to make the old lady responsible.

My client's perception was in fact cock-eyed. Her decision (and it was clearly a matter of choice, since she agreed she could have left any time she wanted to) was to stay, but she was under the delusion that it was all the old lady's fault! How often do we blame others for the choices *we* make? She, too, was not taking responsibility for what she was allowing the old lady to do to her. *Allowing* implies giving permission and it is an important concept in human communication. The effect, of course, is to enhance the power the other person has and to diminish our own.

What was the effect of this new awareness on the two women concerned, you may ask? The first woman cancelled her next appointment, so I only saw her once. I can only assume that she went away a wiser and hopefully a stronger person, intent upon developing her own power within that marriage. The second woman, over a period of time, began to establish her sense of value and worth, with a fresh recognition of her need to withdraw the power she was in the habit of giving to other people. She took this new perception back into her marriage and by taking responsibility for what she had been allowing her husband to do to her over a period of thirty years began to see a transformation. She gave up her image of the helpless victim, prone to every whim or injustice other people handed out to her. She re-established a sense of her own worthwhileness and began to confront her husband about his chauvinist attitudes towards her. The irony was that it was the husband who first asked me to see his wife because of her depression, and he later came to see me to ask what the devil I'd been doing to his wife. The mouse had turned into a lion! There was indeed a stormy period while adjustments were being worked out, but the wife is now no longer depressed and her husband is a wiser man. There has been real growth in place of the gradual deterioration that formerly marked their relationship.

Responsibility, as Fritz Perls[20] once said, is the 'ability to respond: response-ability'. Most of our lives are governed more by what we allow others to do to us than we at first imagine. Seen from the perspective of the invitation or permission we give to others to dictate the way we behave, how can our lives be changed? There needs to be a radical shift from the *abandonment* of responsibility for our lives to an *acceptance* of responsibility. This shift would look like this:

'Abandonment of responsibility' scripts	*'Acceptance of responsibility' scripts*
People are always walking over me.	I'm always letting people walk over me.
My wife won't let me!	I always allow my wife to tell me what I can or cannot do!
He treats me like dirt.	I let him treat me like dirt.
She kept me there five hours!	I let her keep me there for five hours.
She ignores me.	I let her ignore me.
He uses me.	I allow him to use me.
She's making my life a misery!	Somehow I'm giving her permission to ruin my life!

Such alternatives are far from being merely a matter of words.

The words we use betray the ideas and perceptions behind them, and some of those ideas are unhealthy. A relationship in which people are prepared to take full responsibility for themselves, rather than go around blaming others for what they are in fact giving the other person permission to do to them, provides a far healthier model than the 'blaming' one.

There is one further consideration before leaving this subject of responsibility. There are some occasions which prove the exception to this rule. Physical violence, including sexual assault, mugging or rape are often out of our control. I am not for one moment implying that every rape victim, for instance, is responsible for what happens to them. I have counselled too many rape victims to believe that to be true, although much popular (male) mythology still does believe it. There are times and occasions when our freedom of choice is, in fact, physically taken out of our hands and there is not too much we can do about it at the time. I am dealing in this chapter with human *communication* and *relationships*, not physical violence even between couples.

G13. BE SPECIFIC; AVOID GENERALISATIONS.

Among the bad habits we have inherited in our use of language, and often convey in our arguments, is that of 'global' generalisation. The all-inclusive 'everybody', 'men', 'women', 'them', 'all' are often used in a non-specific way, and are therefore too large to handle. 'Everyone says you're a flirt!' is not very helpful in determining just who is saying this. 'That's women for you,' is an obvious over-statement, since the speaker clearly has no experience of 'women' in general, just *some women* in particular.

Similarly, we often use the overworked word 'it' in a non-defined way, which can lead to mystification. 'It's all gone wrong again,' conveys a certain amount of frustration and disappointment, but we are left wondering exactly what 'it' is that has gone wrong. Likewise, 'It's all your fault!' leaves the accused person wondering what exactly is their fault. Responding to such global language is almost impossible, and can result in non-specific accusations being hurled at the other person.

Example: G13.1

HIM: It's all gone wrong again, hasn't it?

HER: What has?
HIM: Oh, you know; everything.
HER: Everything?
HIM: It's never going to change.
HER: Isn't it?
HIM: No, never.
HER: !

To the fly on the wall, this interchange is meaningless, and yet, not a mile from where you are right now, some people are using this kind of language believing that it is communication. Since the original 'it' was never defined, the exchange went downhill from then on.

When we find ourselves in arguments, it helps if we can get the other person to define their global or non-specific statements.

Non-specific statements	Responses inviting specific content
All	Which?
Everyone	Who?
It	What?
Men	Which men?
Women	Which women?
Them	Who?
People	Which people?

One of my former clients was having difficulty in his female relationships. It transpired that his father was killed in the war and he was educated largely through the kindness and generosity of his grandfather. From boarding school my client would go to spend every holiday with his grandfather, until one day he was met on the doorstep and taken for a walk. His grandfather explained that he had remarried, and his new wife did not want the grandson in the house. He never went to stay with his grandfather again and deeply resented this, naturally. My client's woeful comment was, 'Well, that's women for you!' He could equally have said, 'That's grandfathers for you!' – but he didn't. No wonder this global condemnation of 'women' was constantly being projected on to each woman he met (see G14).

We do not have to allow ourselves to be mystified by the vague generalisations which other people use. Before we can make rational responses, we need to know what the other person is meaning. It can be reached this way:

Example G13.2

HIM: Everyone's against me!
HER: Who do you mean by 'everyone'?
HIM: Those people at work.
HER: Which people in particular?
HIM: The bosses.
HER: Any particular boss?
HIM: Mr Hetherington.

By a slow process of definition, narrowing down the original 'everyone', she managed to work through 'people at work' and 'bosses' ending up with Mr Hetherington. Now, his opening statement would sound like, 'Mr Hetherington is against me'.

In arguments which are to do with personal issues between the two parties, each can ask the other for a specific response, like, 'It's OK to tell me what you really think of me without wrapping it up in the opinions of other people' (cf. G8). Or, 'I hear what you say your mother thinks of me, but right now I'm more interested in what *you* think of me.' Non-specific language is very often a way of covering up what we either feel or believe; it is a way of protecting ourselves from making statements ('I' statements) which we might have to own or defend. That is not fighting fair. It is a waste of energy to communicate to another person in a language which is intended to conceal our actual meanings.

G14. DON'T PROJECT YOUR FEELINGS AND IDEAS ON TO OTHER PEOPLE.

Projection is a common means of cloaking how we feel or what we think by *transferring* such feelings or thoughts on to other people. The process of projection can be either conscious or, more often, unconscious.

One aspect of projection has already been noticed in our outline of G11 and G12. 'You make me angry' is a projection of *my* anger on to *you* and making you responsible for it. This is nonsense. I am responsible for my feelings, not you.

The phenomenon of projection is one most frequently used

among the human system of defence mechanisms. Any feelings which we find unacceptable we can attribute to others. My daughter stayed with her grandparents recently, and as soon as she arrived home she dashed upstairs to her bedroom and came down with an armful of dolls. 'They've all been missing me,' she said. In this case, the projection of Katie's feelings on to her dolls is innocent, even charming. But if she is using this projection of her feelings on to her dolls as a means of avoiding the recognition of her own feelings, something more sinister might be going on. 'Perhaps you have been missing them too?' I suggested to Katie, just to make sure!

When couples are arguing, they often resort to this method of projection as a way of *disowning* their feelings (see G11) and blaming the other person for them. From the beginning of time we have habitually found someone to blame for our troubles: our neighbours, our tribe, the other tribe, the Blacks, the Whites, the immigrants, the Reds, etc. 'It's all their fault!' – it is alleged. By projecting our own fears and feelings on to others, we can both escape responsibility for them and also avoid having to deal with them *within ourselves*.

For instance, by projecting hostility and fear concerning homo-sexual feelings within ourselves on to 'them out there' – 'Gays, Queers, Perverts' – we do not have to deal with those fears within ourselves, simply because we have now 'disowned' them and we can deny that they are ours. We can, instead, go out to Clapham Common or wherever and indulge in a bit of 'queer-bashing', venting all our fear, rage and disgust on to the victim (who, by the way, might or might not be 'gay'). It is a way of dealing with our own uncertainties and hostility about ourselves. Instead of loathing ourselves, or that bit of us that is questioning somewhere deep down within us our own sexual orientation, we can loathe the Gays. Instead of hating that bit of us that is dark and shadowy, the 'black' side of our character, we can project all that on to 'the Blacks' (out there) and find in them an object of our hatred, suspicion and fear. In extreme cases of paranoia, individuals can actually disavow quite consciously their own sexual or hostile feelings, and believe that these lie in others. It is now 'them' who have the hostile feelings against *us* or who have sexual designs on *us*.

Another form of projection appears when we project not a hostile feeling but a *need* on to other people, and then try to meet that need by caring for them. The mother who may unconsciously project *her own needs* of nurture on to her child will then over-indulge it, spoil it, and probably try to prevent its growing up into independence. Mothering becomes smothering. Mother's needs become more important than the child's. A further illustration of projecting our needs on to other people is seen in the famous story of the Boy Scout who projects *his* need to help on to the little old lady waiting by the kerbside. In dragging her across the road ('I'm only doing this to help!') he is actually helping himself to feel good and doing his 'good deed' for the day. It is his need *to* help, not the old lady's need *for* help, that is determining this pattern of behaviour.

These methods of projection can destroy relationships. Most of the time they are conveyed quite unconsciously; we do not doubt the sincerity of the Boy Scout – it is his awareness that is sadly lacking.

I recall hearing an argument in a TV programme between a husband and wife which was a well-worn groove concerning his drinking habits; 90 per cent of the time things were fine, but the other 10 per cent was being ruined by his addiction to alcohol. She loathed his drinking. In the process of the argument, he attacked her with a vicious verbal barrage:

> Why then don't you leave? Get out of here, you ass-hole; you're the one who creates all the chaos around here. It was fine until you came in here, messing up my life. I'm sick to death of you and your demands. I wish you'd get the hell out of here, you piss-ant, and leave me alone, for good!

When drunk, this man actually believed that his *wife* was the cause of all his problems, but in attacking her in this way, he was in fact using projection. He projected his 'alcoholic self' on to his wife where he could then attack this side of his own character in the visible form of his wife. (Reread his words above as addressed to his alcoholic self.) It is *alcoholism* that he wants to 'leave' and 'get out'. It is his habitual drinking that 'creates all the chaos around here, messing up my life'. He is in part sick of this anti-social behaviour and its demands on him, and he does wish this nagging need for booze would leave him alone, for good. Unless his wife could 'read' this into his words, she would probably take it all personally, and counter-attack – which on this occasion she did, only to raise the temperature of the row even higher bringing more heat than light.

I remember my mentor, Dr Frank Lake, recalling a dramatic illustration of projection.[21] A client of his was convinced his wife was having an affair. His suspicions were entirely unfounded, and of course she denied it. His obsession finally made him come home several times a day in order to find 'them' together, which of course he never did. 'I know you want a man,' he would say to his wife, and this constant accusation was ruining the whole relationship. Finally, he resorted to physical violence to beat the truth out of her and the result brought both of them into therapy where the problem was exposed. It transpired that (quite unconsciously) the husband was projecting on to the wife *his own needs for a man*, for he was plagued by deeply repressed homosexual fantasies which he found quite impossible to acknowledge, and was actually disgusted by. Once he was able to own his projection the relationship began to improve and the real underlying problem could be dealt with.

In arguments, we do need to keep this aspect of projection in mind and, when we become aware that we are being 'dumped on', to say so. We do not have to allow other people to project their unwanted feelings on to us. A couple who were arguing recently came up against the wife's insistence that the husband 'never really liked me'. No matter what the husband said, he could not convince her that this was untrue. She insisted, elaborating in great detail all the things he disliked about her. 'You can never find anything good in me, can you? You always think the worst,' eventually transpired as the *wife's* script, not the husband's. She was actually addressing not her husband but that bit of herself which was entirely critical of herself. She was projecting on to her husband her own feelings of worthlessness and lack of self-esteem, then blaming *him* for them. The relationship could not possibly improve until this projection was exposed, and owned by the wife.

G15. DON'T STEREOTYPE YOUR PARTNER BY USING DEPERSONALISING LABELS.

Most of us dislike being labelled – being put in a neat little pigeon-hole and described in terms of stereotypes. And yet, most of us go on doing this with other people we meet. We saw in G13 the danger in human relationships of over-generalising, and there is this type of danger whenever we use labels by which to describe other people. It depersonalises them, and reduces them (and us, when we are the recipients) to a mere cypher or 'type'.

The danger of stereotyping is that once we arrive at the 'label' we are going to describe that person by, *we then give up trying to understand them*. We cease to see them as a person capable of being hurt; we see them as a category or type in an impersonal way. There is all the difference in the world between being accepted as a *person* and being recognised as a *type*. Labels reduce our sense of ego-worth. We cease to be seen as a unique human being and, instead, get included among a collective noun where we merely represent what is *typical*. 'The wife' is a commonly used term for a female spouse. By using the definite article (the) rather than the personal 'my', a husband reduces his wife to a *function*, in a rather similar way to the old Church of England Prayer Book Marriage Service, 'I now pronounce you man and wife'. 'Man' goes with 'woman'; 'husband' goes with 'wife'. Man and woman are personal, sexual terms. Husband and Wife are *relational terms* over and above their uniqueness as persons. Equally, 'the old man' is sometimes used as an affectionate term referring to 'my husband', and the same depersonalisation is implicit.

Labels can be used as kinds of diagnostic categories. 'Feminist', 'sadist', 'alcoholic', 'hysteric', 'paranoid' and (most over-done of all) 'neurotic' are useful words in their place, but they are rarely of help when couples argue. They merely enrage, and provoke further retaliatory action. 'You've always been neurotic . . .' is an accusation which will probably be defended, and thus take the couple away from the issue at hand. Strong statements can, and at times should, be made but by using non-labelling techniques. 'You've always hated sex' is a much more defined issue, which can be explored, whereas 'You've always been frigid' tends to reduce the person to a category. Similarly, 'You've always been over-sexed' includes a charge of deviance from the norm (what is the norm?) whereas, 'Sex has always seemed much more important to you than me' is far more accurate as an expression of what *is*. And, put this way, it does invite an adult response rather than a counter-attack simply because the statement does not start out as an attack. Inflammatory statements or accusations simply invite a response in kind.

Relearning our methods of communication will take time and

practice. Here are a few examples of how the new language might sound by way of improving our quality of personal communication:

	Negative: the labelling method	*Positive:* the non-labelling method
1	You're a male chauvinist pig!	I find your putting me down as a woman hard to take and I resent it!
2	Not another of your neurotic outbursts ...	You do seem to be uptight about this – can we talk?
3	Here we go! Turn on the tears – typical female!	Can you tell me what your tears might be saying. I'd really like to hear.
4	You're paranoid!	You sound as if the whole world is against you!
5	You're sick!	That comment sounds sick to me!
6	Typical Northerner/ Southerner!	Do you really believe that, or are you saying it because you were brought up to think that way?
7	You've always been frigid!	You have always seemed to hate sex.

These alternative suggestions are ways of keeping the communication *open*, whereas the labelling statements seem to want to *close down* communication; they appear as 'value-judgements' which are not susceptible of argument or response. In Example 1, the accusation of being an MCP *conceals* the hurt experienced by the hearer, and the suggested non-labelling statement communicates that hurt feeling, as well as the resentment at the speaker's sexist attitude. In Example 2, the focus is kept upon the apparent up-tightness and a willingness to explore this is suggested, rather than dismiss it or judge it in a putting-down fashion. In Example 3, interest focuses upon what the tears are about, rather than upon the dismissive and cynical rejection of those tears implied in the words 'typical female'. (Why should this natural human phenomenon be classified as female, by the way?) Example 4 shows how a response can be made to the inner world of feelings of the other person (who may or may not be clinically paranoid) rather than slap a label on them in an unfeeling and uncaring manner. In Example 5, the distinction is made between the sickness of the person, and the sickness of the remark made by that person. Again, this leaves the recipient free to respond out of their feelings and awareness, as opposed to having to defend against the idea of being sick, e.g. 'Me sick, what about your mother?' etc. In Example 6, global inclusion among the category of a geographical region is avoided by paying attention to upbringing in the matter of ideas and beliefs and concentrates on the questions of choice. In Example 7, the label 'frigid' is avoided but a very strong statement is nevertheless possible without stereotyping the other person. Whereas they might find it hard to respond, understandably, to 'frigid', they might respond otherwise to the more empathic statement about 'hating sex'. They may, in fact, have good reason to do so if, as is sometimes the case, they were sexually abused in childhood.

Non-labelling responses leave the issues open to further discussion and enlightenment; stereotyping merely shuts these down.

G16. BE AWARE OF HOW YOU FEEL INSIDE YOURSELF BEFORE, DURING AND AFTER HEATED ARGUMENTS, AND SHARE THESE FEELINGS WITH YOUR PARTNER.

There are often 'warning signals' before an argument begins, which we would do well to take account of before embarking upon a confrontation with another.

☐ BEFORE: Arguments need not be happenings we just drift into, as if we were helpless victims of some cosmic process. We can often foresee them, sometimes even plan them if they are important enough for us to do so. Instead of drifting, therefore, we could share our awareness of how we feel before we confront, e.g. 'I don't know how this will sound to you, but there is something which I must tell you and I'm nervous about how you will respond to what I have to say.' This is not intended either to intimidate your partner, nor manipulate them into some response they might not want to give. But it is a form of an early warning system, which does declare your own nervousness and vulnerability

– your 'not-sureness'. Sometimes, we need to state the seriousness of our communication, like 'I need to have you listen to me seriously for a moment'. Being honest about what we need gets the dialogue off to an honest and open start (wherever it might end up!) and allows the other person to hear what our need is. Whatever we are feeling at the start of some argument or confrontation, we do have the opportunity of expressing this strongly. 'I feel angry with you and I want to tell you why . . .' at least has the advantage of not starting off with an accusation or by blaming the other person.

□ DURING: In the middle of some arguments, we might come to the awareness that we have got off the point, or some other issue is now occupying the centre of the row. We have the possibility, even in the middle of a heated argument, of saying *how we feel about what is going on*. Like this: 'Wait a minute; I don't like what is going on at the moment; I am feeling confused and angry that we have strayed from my original point, and I'd like to start again.' Or, 'I really don't like the way we're attacking each other right now; can we please get back to the issue?' If our partner is apparently not hearing what we are telling them, it is our responsibility to help them. 'I'm feeling sad that you're not hearing me; I need to know you are hearing what I'm saying. Can you please tell me what I've just been saying?' This way, arguments can be kept 'on track' and not allowed to stray off course. If the person begins to walk away from us, we can respond honestly to that too. 'I really resent your walking away from me right now; I need you to hear what I'm saying and I know this can't be easy for you.' This way we stay in control of the process.

□ AFTER: Some arguments don't go away; they just simmer until the next one. This is because they do not end up to anyone's satisfaction. Take responsibility for how you allow your arguments to end up unsatisfactorily by stating how you see the next course of action. 'As I understand it . . .' or, 'So what we've agreed to is this . . .' Later on, perhaps, you can level with your partner how you felt the argument went. In an honest and real way we can own up to whatever method of 'dirty fighting' we were employing. We can admit that we didn't want to hear this or that, and that we really did want to hurt the other. We can own up to hostile feelings not expressed at the time; this way, we prevent any left-over feelings getting stacked back into the 'ancestral cupboard'

(G7) to await the next confrontation. This style of 'clearing up' pays off. Both partners are clear as to what the row was about, and both are agreed about the next step. Valid points, not admitted during the argument, can often be conceded over coffee afterwards. 'You were absolutely right when you said ... but I hated you for reminding me!' can be a growthful way of communicating to the other person. The important point to remember is to find some return for the energy expended in the process of the argument. An issue resolved, clarification gained, insights acquired and feelings ventilated instead of stifled are all positive gains on offer in order to feed the relationship.

Interlude

So far I have outlined some of the ways in which we may communicate with each other more effectively. We have noticed several times that in some of the traditional ways we speak to each other we do so more in order to conceal what we feel and think than to disclose our inner world. The Guidelines are a constructive model in order to change this state of affairs. Such a change will first of all involve learning a new kind of language, what I call 'Battlespeak' (to coin a phrase reminiscent of George Orwell). Most of us need to come to terms with the idea of constructive aggression and, in place of the bickering, tit-for-tat rituals which are 'full of sound and fury, signifying nothing', to restore the healthy art of quarrelling.

Of course, words alone cannot do this. One early reader of my manuscript raised an important issue when questioning whether people *could* learn to speak as I have suggested throughout the first part of this book. Heaven forbid that the Guidelines should be taken by anyone as a kind of dogmatic Catechism to be learnt by heart and applied unthinkingly! Rather it is the issue behind each of the Guidelines which needs careful thought and which can make our relating to our significant others far more telling. It is my experience among the many couples that I counsel that when they replace their old, unprofitable styles of relating and adopt (in their own words) some of the principles outlined in the Guidelines, significant changes begin to take place. Many of the people I know *have* learnt to make 'I' statements in place of their previously inflammatory 'You' accusations. They find this far more risky, of course, but they also find the benefits worth the risk. Couples *can* learn to take responsibility, to be more direct in communicating their needs, to listen to what the other person is saying and feeling, and to make more appropriate responses. They tell me of the difference this has made to their relationships.

Any means of improving our quality of self-expression in

fighting for our important relationships are better than the sneaky ways which cover up the truth about who we are. Covering-up is a protective method of defence so that we do not have to risk self-exposure to the other person. This will mean challenging the deeper, infantile scripts we have inherited aimed at half-truth and the 'thou-shalt-not-upset-thy-neighbour' indoctrination.

In the next part of the book, I shall attempt to illustrate how the Guidelines might work out in practice. The means I shall use comprises some extended dialogues between couples, drawing on some common themes found in marital counselling. The couples are, of course, entirely fictitious. First, I shall introduce the issue or theme in their argument, and the context of their relationship. Then will follow an imaginary dialogue between the couple which will disclose their style of arguing. A further section will contain an extended analysis of what is going on between the two people, pointing out their hidden agendas and things of which they themselves might be completely unaware but which constitute an important ingredient in their argument. I do not claim that my analyses are exhaustive, and I hope that you might be able to spot other things that are going on between the couples besides the ones I draw to your attention. The eight couples are entirely representative of a much wider variety of people and situations.

Part Two
GUIDELINES
IN ACTION

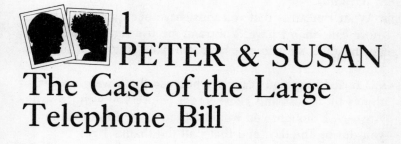

1
PETER & SUSAN
The Case of the Large Telephone Bill

Susan has quite a history of running up large telephone bills and it's been a regular cause of discussion and argument between her and Peter, her live-in boy-friend. Peter has the distinct impression that Susan believes money grows on trees. She has, he often says jokingly, champagne tastes with Guinness money. Less jokingly, Susan has a fierce temper which often renders Peter speechless and afraid. No matter where an argument starts, it usually ends up with Peter in the doghouse and an atmosphere you could cut with a knife.

In spite of this, they were attached to each other and at times there were periods of closeness. Susan had maintained that their biggest problem was they were not living together, and that if they were most of their difficulties would disappear. Peter wasn't quite convinced about this, but he did agree to give it a try, and Susan moved in a few months ago. Occasionally, his mind turned to the wisdom of his decision and he wondered how this would affect his very limited finances. One day the telephone account arrived, confirming his worst fears. He doesn't want to upset the relationship which is going well at present, but neither does he want large bills coming in that he is unable to meet. Without thinking about it, his feelings suddenly erupted.

PETER: Bloody hell!

SUSAN: What's wrong?

PETER: It's the telephone bill. It's gone up to over a hundred quid.

SUSAN: Well, I hope you're not going to accuse me of that. I'm not the only one in this house, remember?

PETER: But it's never been this big before. *I* haven't been using the 'phone three times as much.

SUSAN: Meaning?

PETER: What I mean is that you must have been making a lot more calls than I have. You rang me five times yesterday, for instance, so who else have you been ringing, I'd like to know.

SUSAN: Look, I rang you yesterday because there were important things to discuss and I just forgot before you went to work. Anyway, I thought you would like to know I'm thinking of you during the day, and that's all the thanks I get.

PETER: If you'd only write down things that are important, you'd only have to ring me up once, not five times! You do this when we go shopping. You never have a list, then you expect me to go running back to the supermarket because you've forgotten half the shopping.

SUSAN: That was just because you said we had to get back for the baby-sitter; it was *you* that rushed me, no wonder I got flustered and forgot things.

PETER: Well, we had no baby-sitter to get back to when you forgot to take the baby to the doctor when it had that rash last week. I asked you to take him, and when I got back you said you'd just forgot. Probably you were too busy on the 'phone to your mother to remember!

SUSAN: Well, it's not my fault that I forget sometimes. We can all do that, you know. What about you when you ... (*and so on and so on ...*).

This argument can go on for ever, round and round in circles but getting nowhere. An analysis of this style of arguing shows what is happening under the surface.

Script	*Analysis*
P1 Bloody hell!	
S1 What's wrong?	
P2 It's the telephone bill. It's gone up to over £100.	Peter expresses his concern.
S2 Well, I hope you're not going to accuse me of that.	Susan goes on to the defensive here, anticipating P's attack. What is it she fears? Her inner fear blocks out P's own feelings of concern so they get unacknowledged.
I'm not the only one in this house, remember?	By attempting to *deflect* blame on to P (but in an indirect way, notice) S is abandoning any responsibility on her part for the increase in the telephone bill.
P3 But it's never been this big before. I haven't been using the 'phone three times as much!	P is trying to express his real concern at this debt but also in an *indirect* manner; he is responding to S's defensiveness with some of his own. She says, 'I'm not responsible,' so he follows suit.
S3 Meaning?	S invites P to unpack his last comment in a more direct manner.
P4 What I mean is you must have been making a lot more calls than I have.	P now makes the accusation *directly*. The statement is reinforced by his not having had his original feelings of anxiety responded to.
You rang me five times yesterday, for example, so who	P now cites examples to back up his case against S. By now, he's

59

else have you been ringing, I'd like to know?

convinced this large bill is 'all her fault'. They are confronting one another, not the problem of the payment of the bill.

S4 Look, I rang you yesterday because there were important things to discuss and I just forgot before you went to work.

S still on the defensive and starting up the excuses ('just because'). She does not appear to connect these five 'phone calls with the size of the bill!

Anyway, I thought you would like to know I'm thinking of you during the day, and that's all the thanks I get.

An olive branch! Again, no awareness of how she has contributed to P's sense of shock.

P5 If you'd only write down things that are important you'd only have to ring me up once, not five times!

P fails to respond to S's olive branch, so her feelings too are ignored here. He starts to lecture her instead.

You do this when we go shopping. You never have a list, then you expect me to go running back to the supermarket because you've forgotten half the shopping!

Now P starts to raid the 'ancestral cupboard' of their relationship. Old resentments now begin to emerge. Because they have not been dealt with in the past, they still smoulder deep within P and he now finds an appropriate moment to express them.

S5 That was just because you said we had to get back for the baby-sitter; it was you that rushed me; no wonder I got flustered and forgot things.

Again, there is no awareness on S's part of any responsibility for her own actions. They are all P's fault! By this time the 'phone bill is out of sight, and P and S are going over the smouldering ashes of past unfinished encounters. She is still excusing herself ('just because').

P6 Well, we had no baby-sitter to get back to when you forgot to take the baby to the doctor when it had that rash last week. I asked you to take him, and when

Still more from the ancestral cupboard. P obviously feels strongly about this scenario of S's memory but is not expressing his feelings to her.

I got back, you said you'd 'just forgot'.

He is scoring points. The matter of the visit to the doctor was not dealt with adequately *at the time*, or maybe his feelings were expressed then but went unheard. Anyway, they provide more ammunition for the slanging match.

Probably you were too busy on the 'phone to your mother to remember!

Ouch! P now goes for the jugular vein. First, he uses sarcasm which is a veiled form of his anger. Secondly, he brings into the argument S's mother – an obvious source of contention. This is dirty fighting, and they're in for a long night of it . . .

S6   Well, it's not my fault that I forget sometimes. We can all do that you know. What about *your* mother when she forgot my birthday last year . . .

A pathetic abandonment from S's inner 'child' of any responsibility for her actions (there is a clear character defect underneath this phenomenon). S pathetically appeals to human nature and memory but it's a generalisation and not pertinent to what they are saying. Accusation and counter-accusation now follow. It's getting nowhere. They are into old unresolved conflicts, and the issue of the 'phone bill will be just one more to add to the pile when the next row breaks out.

Meanwhile, next door . . .

2
RON & BETTY
Another Case of a Large Telephone Bill

Ron and Betty, who live next door to Susan and Peter, have also received their telephone bill this morning. It, too, has gone up appreciably, and this coincides with Betty's recent arrival. . . !

RON: Bloody hell!
BETTY: What's the matter?
RON: The telephone bill; it's gone up to over £100!
BETTY: My usual bill was always around that – but it seems this is much more than your usual bill. You've gone as white as a sheet!
RON: Gone up? It's twice as much!
BETTY: Well, I suppose it was bound to go up, Ron, with two adults now using the 'phone – not to mention our baby-sitter.
RON: Our budget can't afford bills like these.
BETTY: I know that, Ron. Look, it's nearly time for work. Let's look at this again tonight.

Later . . .

RON: Regarding that bill, Betty. I felt angry this morning and I wanted to shift all the blame on to you. I know that's not fair, but over £100! I've been worried stiff all day. I don't know where I can find this sort of money.
BETTY: It's 'we' now, you know, not 'I'. Remember I'm sharing the house with you and that means the bills too. I don't earn much from my part-time job, but I'll certainly chip in and see how much I can find.
RON: Thanks, Betty. I'd forgotten about that 'we' for a moment. I suppose it's 'our' bill now, isn't it?
BETTY: Yes. I admit I've been gassing on the blower a bit since I moved in. I wanted to tell everyone about my move, and

how good things were now between us. I must have
overdone it, I guess. Sorry if I've given you a shock.

RON: Thanks. It might help, I suppose, if we set a kind of budget
for the 'phone, and try to keep within it. There's always
the standing charge, of course, but we could try and keep
the units down if we used the 'phone after 1 p.m. and
made non-urgent calls after 6.

BETTY: OK. I tell you what. Why don't I put a sticker on the
handset saying 'Is this urgent?' – just to remind us?

RON: Sounds like a good idea to me, Betty. That way, we'll both
remember not to run up bills like this again.

Ron and Betty's way of dealing with the large telephone bill is
quite obviously different from that of Peter and Susan. But initially
they are all dealing with a similar problem, a large rise in the
account. Ron and Betty have found a different and more constructive way of dealing with this problem, however, and in the following
analysis we shall see that they were applying some of the insights
we have already outlined in the Guidelines to Effective
Communication.

Script	Analysis
R1 Bloody hell!	
B1 What's the matter?	
R2 The telephone bill; it's gone up to over £100!	
B2 My usual bill was always around that –	Betty's experience is quite different from that of Ron,
but it seems this is much more than your usual bill. You've gone as white as a sheet.	but she is able to hear Ron's sense of shock and to respond to it. This is an empathic response, that is, she is able to tune in to what Ron is feeling, and to reflect this back to him so he feels that he is heard.
R3 Gone up? It's twice as much!	Since Betty is clearly hearing him he can go on exploring the impact of the bill.

B3 Well, I suppose it was bound to go up, Ron, with two adults now using the 'phone – not to mention the baby-sitter.

Unlike Susan who immediately defended and covered up, Betty is able to appeal to reason. This brings out the new situation which has brought about the increase in the 'phone bill, and also brings Ron out of any fantasies he might have about all the household bills being the same as they were in the past.

R4 Our budget can't afford bills like these.

An open and honest expression, free of blame or recrimination.

B4 I know that, Ron.

Betty is in agreement with Ron. Free of blame, this inter-action enables them both to listen to one another more deeply.

Look, it's nearly time for work. Let's look at this again tonight.

A realistic way of ending this part of their dialogue with a view to further thought later. They gain space for reflection.

Later

R5 Regarding that bill, Betty. I felt angry this morning and I wanted to shift all the blame on to you. I know that's not fair, but over £100!

Ron now levels with Betty about the feelings which did not get expressed earlier. He shares these angry feelings together with his temptation to put the blame on her. He can now reassess his first reaction while still owning his sense of shock and worry.

I've been worried stiff all day – I don't know where I can find this sort of money.

Ron is not busy trying to protect Betty from his feelings; instead of cloaking his anxiety by denial or blame, he shares this worry openly.

B5 It's 'we' now, you know, not 'I'. Remember, I'm sharing the house with you and that means the bills too.

Betty raises Ron's awareness by reminding him that he is not expected to face these bills alone; she is able to stay close to his anxiety without labelling it as silly, etc.

	I don't earn much from my part-time job, but I'll certainly chip in and see how much I can find.	A practical contribution to solving the problem. Notice that R and B are beginning to tackle the problem, not each other.
R6	Thanks, Betty. I'd forgotten about that 'we' for a moment. I suppose it's our bill now, isn't it?	Ron received Betty's attempt to raise his awareness of togetherness, and her offer of help. He is honest about what he had overlooked.
B6	Yes. I admit I've been gassing on the blower a bit since I moved in. I wanted to tell everyone about my move, and how good things are now between us. I must have overdone it, I guess.	Betty can now make her honest admission of her contribution to the size of the account. She is able to do this in an atmosphere free of blame and intimidation.
	Sorry if I've given you a shock.	Betty shows she is not unaware of the effect of this bill on Ron and again reminds him she has heard his feelings.
R7	Thanks. It might help, I suppose, if we set a kind of budget for the 'phone, and try to keep within it. There's always the standing charge, of course, but we could try and keep the units down if we used the 'phone after 1 p.m. and made non-urgent calls after 6?	Ron acknowledges Betty's share of the responsibility. He can now concentrate on the problem of the bills in future. He puts forward some practical suggestions and uses the freshly discovered 'we' as an indication that this is a shared activity and concern.
B7	OK. I tell you what. Why don't we put a sticker on the handset, saying 'Is this urgent?' – just to remind us?	Betty picks up Ron's attempt to tackle the problem by a contribution of her own.
R8	Sounds like a good idea to me, Betty. That way, we'll both remember not to run up bills like this again.	Ron makes a positive response to Betty's idea and they are now both aware of the potential problem and how to avoid it in the future.

Here, then, are two different couples who are tackling a similar problem: spending money. Such financial matters are by no means insignificant in starting quarrels between partners. While Peter and Susan spent their energy tackling each other, trying to pin the blame on to one another (as if that would pay the bill!), Ron and Betty illustrate a more constructive method of using energy in confronting the real problem. They appear to be able to listen to each other at a greater depth than Peter and Susan who threaten and blame their way through the dialogue getting nowhere. Their ancestral cupboard was being opened to bring out old, unresolved problems; if they have one, at least Ron and Betty did not resort to opening it on this occasion.

3
PAULA & STEVE
The Affair – I

Paula and Steve have been married for 15 years. They have two sons, aged 12 and 10. Paula is a teacher at a secondary modern school and Steve is an insurance salesman. Recently they have been having problems in their relationship which focus mainly on Steve's late home-coming. Steve appears to Paula to have been too busy and their times together have been getting less and less. Steve has appeared evasive about his movements, and rather tetchy and withdrawn, almost preoccupied. Paula has begun to wonder if there is another woman involved and, feeling rather nervous, decides to tackle Steve about his behaviour . . .

STEVE: (*arriving home very late*)
PAULA: Do you realise what time this is?
STEVE: Got to have a late pass, have I?
PAULA: Well, where have you been? You can't have been making calls up to this hour!
STEVE: You make me sick, you do! I come home after working all hours to find you with a face as long as a fiddle!
PAULA: And whose fault is that, I'd like to know! You're never here half the time – I never see you.
STEVE: That's right, it's all my fault, I suppose?
PAULA: I'd still like to know where you've been.
STEVE: Nowhere special.
PAULA: What does that mean?
STEVE: What's this inquisition about, anyway?
PAULA: You know as well as I do, Steve, that you've been coming home later each week. I hardly see you, working all hours. We never seem to speak – and I'd like to know what's wrong.
STEVE: Well, you don't suppose that coming home to you has been a bundle of laughs lately, do you?
PAULA: Are you seeing someone else?

STEVE: Someone else?

PAULA: You know – another woman.

STEVE: (*after a pause*) Well, if you must know, yes, there is. You were bound to find out sooner or later anyway.

PAULA: I knew it! Who is she?

STEVE: What difference does it make?

PAULA: I'd still like to know.

STEVE: A girl at the office.

PAULA: (*after a silence*) I'll put the kettle on. You and I have a lot to talk about, Steve.

This marriage has clearly reached a crisis point. By the time the eternal triangle emerges much damage has already been done, and Steve and Paula need to sort out their feelings about one another and to share what each sees as the future of the marriage relationship. Is it dead, or just wounded? Affairs do not have to lead to an inevitable ending of a marriage. Very often they arise out of a vacuum within the existing relationship, whereby an emotional 'shopping list' of unmet needs goes unattended. Perhaps an analysis of Steve and Paula's arguing style might reveal some of the issues which underlie this particular crisis.

	Script	Analysis
S1	(*arriving home very late*)	
P1	Do you realise what time this is?	In this interchange between Steve and Paula, no less than nine responses are questions. In G2 we saw how questions often *conceal* feelings, and this is true of S and P.
S2	Got to have a late pass, have I?	One question is 'answered' by another. Just as Paula conceals her feelings of concern or anger, Steve here tries to deflect P's unspoken feelings by sarcasm, thus concealing his anger at P's question.
P2	Well, where have you been? You can't have been making calls up to this hour!	P still conceals her feelings, but now tries to disarm S's anticipated excuses of 'working

late'. Steve therefore feels
cornered and lets P know this.

S3	You make me sick, you do! I come home after working all hours to find you with a face as long as a fiddle!	S is clearly unsettled by P's questioning and decides to counter-attack as the best means of defence. This is a variation of the denial of responsibility, turning this back as 'all your fault' and giving as a pathetic reason the length of P's face! He fails to connect P's sadness with his own behaviour.
P3	And whose fault is that, I'd like to know!	P refuses to accept S's implied blame and tries to raise S's awareness as to his part in her sense of sadness.
	You're never here half the time – I never see you.	Playing the 'blaming game', P directly attributes her feelings to S. There is still no *direct* confession to inner feelings.
S4	That's right, it's all my fault, I suppose?	S picks up, correctly, P's blaming him for how she feels. His question *conceals* the statement which lies behind it, viz. I'm not prepared to take all the blame.
P4	I'd still like to know where you've been.	P brings the subject back to the beginning and tries again to get a straight answer from S.
S5	Nowhere special.	Simple evasion, and (as we see later on) also a lie!
P5	What does that mean?	P does not confront S directly, but chooses rather to continue with her questioning technique. She conceals her rising frustration.
S6	What's this inquisition about, anyway?	Another question! S, tries to belittle P by his use of 'inquisition'. This is his way of

saying, 'Leave it alone,' because P is clearly pursuing a subject behind which S has very strong *feelings*. They are both sparring with each other, circling round and round without landing a 'blow' yet. They are both trying to find a gap in the other's defences.

P6   You know as well as I do, Steve, that you've been coming home later each week.

P decides to bring the subject out into the open and begins to argue now more directly concerning S's behaviour.

I hardly see you, working all hours.

This means: I miss you, but P can't bring herself to say this. Thus she is concealing her feelings.

We never seem to speak – and I'd like to know what's wrong.

Again, this is all cerebral and factual. P persists in her search for information, and now invites S to explain himself.

S7   Well, you don't suppose that coming home to you has been a bundle of laughs lately, do you?

Yet another evasive question. S seems almost incapable of giving a straight answer to any of P's questions. One question follows another. He implies yet again that it is P's fault he comes home late.

P7   Are you seeing someone else?

P now decides to confront S directly. She has been hoping he would tell her why he comes home late, and she is now forced to declare her inner fears by yet another question.

S8   Someone else?

Further evasion, as if S does not understand P's question. He is still covering up like the artful dodger he is!

P8   You know – another woman?

P spells it out clearly.

S9	*(after a pause)* Well, if you must know, yes, there is. You were bound to find out sooner or later, anyway.	The truth at last! S decides to tell P that her fears and suspicions are well founded and her instincts correct. There is just a hint of relief in his voice.
P9	I knew it! Who is she?	Relief and fear combine in this statement as she probes further.
S10	What difference does it make?	More reluctance to tell all the truth.
P10	I'd still like to know.	P needs to know who it is she is now competing with.
S11	A girl at the office.	The rival is a 'girl', i.e. younger than P.
P11	*(after a silence)* I'll put the kettle on. You and I have a lot to talk about, Steve.	Time out to reflect on the implications of this confession by S.

Whatever might have been going on in Steve and Paula's relationship, owning up to what they were feeling individually does not appear to have been a characteristic. They each conceal their feelings behind questions and a search for information and explanation. The deeper matters of the heart are left unacknowledged, although somewhere in both of these people there seems to be much pain and unhappiness. This exchange, therefore, illustrates the point we made in G9 concerning the phenomenon of nagging which, when it becomes a kind of generalised hostility, disguises the precise and particular needs of the nagger. Paula starts out this way, and Steve correctly picks up the hostility in the tone and questioning of his wife. Feeling under attack (which he does not acknowledge directly) he tries to blame Paula for his emotional and physical withdrawal.

This interaction illustrates how couples often conduct their relationship along the sidelines of the playing field of life. Or, if the relationship is likened to a circle, some couples keep to the circumference where only day-to-day matters are ever discussed, those things which must be talked about to keep the routine of the household going. They never (or seldom) go to the heart of the matter, the centre of the circle, where feelings lie buried but not forgotten. Unresolved conflicts build up, but are not expressed *directly*. However, they do find *indirect* expression by an unfocused frustration as in Paula's case. This couple has allowed issues to remain undisclosed and unexplored until, almost inevitably, a crisis such as Steve's affair takes the lid off the pot. Fairly typically, the affair challenges the whole structure of Paula and Steve's marriage and they must now go on to assess whether or not their union is salvageable.

4
MIKE & BRENDA
The Affair – II

Among the many crises which couples will almost inevitably have to face within their relationship, none is potentially more explosive than 'the affair'. The reason is not hard to find. Since relationships are, if they are to grow and find breathing spaces, based on trust and commitment, an affair by one of the partners strikes at the very heart of the relationship. Something which both parties either agreed or assumed to be the case (for instance, sexual fidelity) has been violated. An analysis of the *causes* of such affairs lies outside our present concern. We shall concentrate on how this kind of severe blow to the relationship can be ventilated using some of the Guidelines to effective communication we outlined in Part I. Reactions to the news of an 'affair', and indeed to the manner in which it is discovered, vary considerably. For the purpose of illustrating some of these reactions, let us reconstruct the conversation between the 'girl at the office' with whom Steve in our previous section was involved (her name is Brenda, by the way) and her husband Mike.

The scene is the home of Mike and Brenda. They have been married for about five years, and have no children. Financially, they need two salaries in paying off the house and building up their home. Mike is a regional manager of a chain of garages and his work takes him away from home quite a lot. Brenda works for Steve's firm of Insurers. Steve has now told Brenda that Paula knows of their affair and it has to end. Brenda decides to level with Mike at the first opportunity.

MIKE: That was a super meal, love.
BRENDA: Was it (*vaguely*)?
MIKE: You've been quiet all evening. Is everything OK?
BRENDA: No, Mike, everything is not OK. Come and sit down.
    I need to talk about it.
MIKE: Fire away!

BRENDA: I'm afraid I've got something to say to you and I know you aren't going to like what it is. I feel dreadful.

MIKE: What is it?

BRENDA: I've been seeing this man at the office . . . I never intended it to go anywhere . . . it's all so stupid really . . .

MIKE: Look, Brenda. Take your time and tell me the story from the beginning.

BRENDA: One of the men in my office is called Steve. He's married. He asked me out for a drink after work one day when you were away. He's pleasant enough and I thought, 'Why not?'

MIKE: Then what?

BRENDA: We had so much in common. We had a similar sense of humour and it was nice to sit and chat. I think before either of us knew it something else began to happen. I started looking forward to seeing him and enjoying how I felt with him. I seemed important to him. He seemed to appreciate my company. It went on from there.

MIKE: How far?

BRENDA: One night I suppose we both had a bit too much to drink, and we ended up having sex in his car. It sounds so sordid to say this in the cold light of day. I feel so desperately ashamed . . . (*cries*).

MIKE: I can't believe this! You, of all people! I hear of this kind of thing happening to some of my employees and I've always thought, 'Never my Brenda'. I just don't believe it!

BRENDA: You sound shocked!

MIKE: Shocked? That's the understatement of the year! I'm devastated! It's the deceit as much as anything else. Carrying on behind my back while I'm away. I feel thoroughly betrayed. Why the hell didn't you tell me what was going on before this thing got too involved?

BRENDA: I didn't want to hurt your feelings.

MIKE: Hurt my feelings? Well what the hell do you suppose you have done now, eh? Am I supposed to say, 'That's OK love; what's on telly?'

BRENDA: No, of course not. I'd like you to tell me exactly what you're feeling about this. I hear you're angry and you're entitled to feel that. I'd feel just as mad if I were in your shoes.

MIKE: Feelings? I'll tell you what I'm feeling. I'm feeling I've been made a bloody fool of, that's what I'm feeling. I'm furious with you . . . and him. All that we've worked for and dreamed of – now, finished! You've seen to that! How could you?

BRENDA: If either of us is a bloody fool, Mike, it's me. I can't stand to see you hurt like this. And it's all my fault.

MIKE: What on earth possessed you?

BRENDA: I don't want to make excuses, Mike, but I hardly know myself. Looking back, I know I was missing you when you had to stay overnight with your work. I just never said so. I guess I was flattered by Steve and never quite realised how I'd been missing having attention paid to me. I just buried it all.

MIKE: So now it's all my fault, is it, because I've been working hard to pay for all this?

BRENDA: That's not what I meant, Mike. I'm trying to tell you about some of the things I've been missing in our relationship recently and which I'd never told you about. I wish to God I had!

MIKE: So while we're on the subject, what other things aren't you happy about. We might as well have them *all* out in the open.

BRENDA: I've lost the sense that I matter to you, Mike. I know you love me. But you seem so wrapped in your work, often bringing it home at night. I seem to be a piece of furniture at times – familiar, and in my place, but not really important. I see now it was wrong of me not to say something sooner, but I'm saying it now, Mike. I need to see more of you, and I don't mean on the other side of your brief case!

MIKE: All right! I'll review my work-load and try to be more available.

BRENDA: Thanks, and maybe you'll come to bed a little less tired. You must have noticed that our sex life has dropped to zero recently.

MIKE: No, I hadn't realised that. You never said . . .

BRENDA: Well, I'm saying it now. And in future I'm going to be more honest with you about what I need, and miss. I've tried to protect you too much, and I've ended up hurting you even more.

MIKE: I do hurt. By the way; is it over? Between thingummy and
you I mean?

BRENDA: Yes, it's over. I want to use my energies now in healing
this rift between you and me. I do love you, Mike. And
I'm so sorry, so sorry . . .

MIKE: It'll take time, but maybe we've enough love and honesty
left to make it happen.

Now, in more detail let's examine this couple's style of arguing:

Script	Analysis
M1 That was a super meal, love.	
B1 Was it (*vaguely*)?	
M2 You've been quiet all evening.	Mike shares his awareness . . .
Is everything OK?	. . . and invites Brenda to share her own.
B2 No, Mike, everything is not OK.	B does not have to cover up her feelings and thus can affirm M's awareness as correct.
Come and sit down. I need to talk about it.	B clears the 'stage' in order to spend time discussing the pending crisis. Notice B expresses *her* need to talk about 'it' directly, and does not resort to denial or avoidance.
M3 Fire away!	
B3 I'm afraid I've got something to say to you and I know you aren't going to like what it is. I feel dreadful.	B prepares M for the shock. She expresses her feelings of fear and dread well aware of the importance of what she has to say.
M4 What is it?	M does not waste time trying to guess at what B is about to say. He asks her directly.
B4 I've been seeing this man at the office . . .	B's anxiety finds expression in her disjointed sentences, not quite knowing where to start.
I never intended it to go anywhere . . .	B clearly does not regard the affair as in any way permanent.

76

it's all so stupid really . . .

B gets off the track and starts to censor her behaviour before she has told M what it is. So . . .

M5 Look, Brenda. Take your time and tell me the story from the beginning.

M invites B to tell her story. M shows remarkable patience here by not jumping in with his own conclusions *before* he knows all the facts.

B5 One of the men in my office is called Steve. He's married. He asked me out for a drink after work one day when you were away. He's pleasant enough and I thought, 'Why not?'

The story is unfolded . . .

M6 Then what?

M is listening at this stage and naturally wants to know where this story is going.

B6 We had so much in common. We had a similar sense of humour and it was nice to sit and chat.

I think before either of us knew it something else began to happen. I started looking forward to seeing him and to how I felt with him. I seemed important to him. He seemed to appreciate my company. It went on from there.

There is some nostalgia in what B is saying – what had been lacking in her marriage for her to feel this way? Through either ignorance or neglect, a vacuum appears to have formed which Steve was available to fill.

M7 How far?

M is listening to B, and picks up her phrase of 'went on'. He dares to ask what he fears to hear.

B7 One night I suppose we both had a bit too much to drink, and we ended up having sex in his car.

A painfully honest confession without resorting to excuses or blame.

It sounds so sordid to say this in the cold light of day.

This is B's adult awareness and her honest description of her own behaviour.

I feel so desperately ashamed
... (*cries*).

B shares with M her deepest
feelings of shame at what she
has done and freely vents those
feelings through her tears ...

M8 I can't believe this!

Now it is M's turn to vent his
feelings about what he has
heard. His first awareness is one
of shock and disbelief ...

You, of all people!

It would be interesting to know
where M is coming from in this
statement. Did he think B was
immune from the notice of
other men?

I hear of this kind of thing
happening to some of my
employees and I've always
thought, 'Never my Brenda'. I
just don't believe it!

M's basic assumption has been
shattered, as has his trust in her
fidelity. He hears what she says,
but part of him can't yet allow
the full force of this affair to
reach him. He struggles with
the truth.

B8 You sound shocked!

B is fully in touch with the
reality of M's feelings and is not
backing away from his own
emotional reaction.

M9 Shocked? That's the
understatement of the year! I'm
devastated!

B's response in B8 enables M
to go further into his inner
feelings. Notice how close they
really are in this interaction,
staying with the feelings of the
other.

It's the deceit as much as
anything else. Carrying on
behind my back while I'm away.
I feel thoroughly betrayed.

The shock is abating, and now
awareness of betrayal by B
emerges.

Why the hell didn't you tell me
what was going on before this
thing got too involved?

M moved away from his feelings
here into a need for
explanations and information.
M rightly feels hurt by B's
silence ...

B9 I didn't want to hurt your feelings.

An uncharacteristic and pathetic cliché from B. She is unaware of (or concealing) the fact of her own need to protect *herself* by her silence.

M10 Hurt my feelings? Well what the hell do you suppose you have done now, eh?

B's attempt in B9 to excuse her silence under the guise of protecting M gets the response it deserves. It simply made matters worse for M, not better. He does not hide his pain from B.

Am I supposed to say, 'That's OK love; what's on telly?'

M now disengages from his feelings and resorts to sarcasm to conceal his anger. In using the word 'supposed' he implies even in his sarcasm that there is a proper way in which he 'ought' to respond.

B10 No, of course not.

B does not respond to M's veiled invitation to be told what he 'ought' to say. She rejects the very idea. Rather ...

I'd like you to tell me exactly what you're feeling about this.

... B invites M to express his true feelings ...

I hear you're angry and you're entitled to feel that. I'd feel just as mad if I were in your shoes.

... and reflects to M what she is aware of in terms of his own anger. She accepts his anger and his right to be angry, and her openness to M is confirmed by her ability to begin to identify with his feelings if she were in his shoes. This is called empathy.

M11 Feelings? I'll tell you what I'm feeling. I'm feeling I've been made a bloody fool of, that's what I'm feeling.

This is not a feeling at all! M merely discloses an opinion about himself. Of course, there *is* an emotion underneath this opinion, which might appropriately be that of *humiliation*. His use of 'been made' hints at what he regards as B's responsibility for how he feels.

I'm furious with you ... and him.

M resumes contact with his feelings and does not attempt to protect B from them. He also realises that some of his fury is for Steve.

All that we've worked for and dreamed of – now, finished! You've seen to that! How could you?

A further emotion comes to the surface here, that of sadness. It is often the case that in men, anger comes first, then sadness, whereas in women it is often the other way round. M is now more reflective about the long-term results of this affair ...

B11 If either of us is a bloody fool, Mike, it's me.

A full acceptance of responsibility by B for the present crisis, and an acknowledgement of her folly.

I can't stand to see you hurt like this. And it's all my fault.

B is able to reach out into M's pain and bravely to acknowledge her culpability.

M12 What on earth possessed you?

The more immediate reaction of hurt and anger now gives way to a preparation for understanding and integration of this event into their marriage.

B12 I don't want to make excuses, Mike, but I hardly know myself. Looking back, I know I was missing you when you had to stay overnight with your work. I just never said so.

B starts to recall some of the precipitating factors which led up to her noticing (and being noticed by) Steve. The 'gap' in the relationship is now being examined. B takes responsibility for her silence in not levelling with M.

I guess I was flattered by Steve and never quite realised how I'd been missing having attention paid to me. I just buried it all.

B is honest about how important Steve's flattery was to her. B was being overlooked by M in the past, but never verbalised it. It got buried, but buried alive!

M13 So now it's all my fault, is it, because I've been working hard to pay for all this?

M mishears B, illustrating his need to exonerate himself from *any* responsibility for what has taken place. He needs to hear what B is trying to say to him, and taking her part of this responsibility invites him to do the same.

B13 That's not what I meant, Mike. I'm trying to tell you about some of the things I've been missing in our relationship recently, and which I've never told you about. I wish to God I had!

This evening is clearly a moment of truth for both B and M. B confronts M's comment at M13 and invites M to hear her correctly. Again, she takes responsibility for her silences in the past and now tries to rectify this.

M14 So while we're on the subject, what other things aren't you happy about? We might as well have them *all* out in the open.

M now dares to ask B to declare other things she has not spoken about. The ancestral cupboard is about to be emptied!

B14 I've lost the sense that I matter to you, Mike.

B confesses to her loss of self-worth for which she is ready to take some of the blame as in B13.

I know you love me.

A reminder of the bedrock on which both B and M are trying to rebuild trust and hope.

But you seem so wrapped up in your work, often bringing it home at night.

I seem to be a piece of furniture at times – familiar, and in my place, but not really important.

A picture of depersonalisation.

I see now it was wrong of me not to say something sooner, but I'm saying it now, Mike. I need to see more of you, Mike, and I don't mean on the other side of your brief case!

Here is a direct expression of B's needs, and notice they relate to Mike, not Steve. The latter was not the *cause* of the affair, merely the *occasion* for it. The cause now emerges to be a mixture of unmet needs and

		silence, both providing a powerful explosive.
M15	All right! I'll review my work-load and try to be more available.	M accepts B's need, and agrees to adjust his time-table to meet it. A constructive offer.
B15	Thanks, and maybe you'll come to bed a little less tired. You must have noticed that our sex life has dropped to zero recently.	M's offer is accepted and now linked to another result of M's work-load, namely his tiredness. It is this that B sees as directly related to her unmet sexual needs.
M16	No, I hadn't realised that. You never said ...	M acknowledges his lack of awareness.
B16	Well, I'm saying it now. And in future I'm going to be more honest with you about what I need, and miss.	B uses her adult awareness to communicate to M. She is not going to wait for her needs to be met; she is going to bring them to M's attention.
	I've tried to protect you too much, and I've ended up hurting you even more.	An astonishing piece of enlightenment! B has learned the lesson not to protect her spouse from her feelings.
M17	I do hurt.	M is not afraid to stay with the reality of his pain, free of blame.
	By the way; is it over? Between thingummy and you I mean?	Hardly 'by the way' – a crucial concern hides behind the apparent casualness of this question!
B17	Yes, it's over. I want to use my energies now in healing this rift between you and me.	M is assured, and B realises that there is a long way to go in the healing process this crisis has provoked.
	I do love you, Mike. And I'm sorry, so sorry ...	The reality of B's love for M is affirmed – a longer-lasting reality than her fling with Steve. Again, she makes an unqualified apology.
M18	It'll take time, but maybe we've	M is aware of the resources they

enough love and honesty left to make it happen.

both have to make a fresh start. He knows (as B does in B17) that the process is not yet finished, but they are both aware in each other of the willingness to heal the break in their relationship.

Mike and Brenda illustrate a contrasting style of arguing from Steve and Paula. The latter are characterised by evasion, blaming and concealment. Mike and Brenda use different techniques, namely, honesty, direct expression of feelings and the willingness to hear the feelings of the other, and a free, non-blaming, expression of those feelings. Mike and Brenda have learned to risk sharing their inner feelings and needs, although Brenda comes to understand in this scenario how she had started to protect Mike from her needs thus setting up the almost inevitability of her affair. This couple have the ability of *listening* to each other, and of taking their full share of responsibility for the *status quo*. Feelings do not have to be reined in before growth in their marriage can appear; their expression is indeed a mark that there already exists in their relationship the ability to grow.

Try rereading these two contrasting dialogues, and discover for yourself the kind of things you are in the habit of saying in your own style of arguing. You may find some alternative responses which can help you to change what might be a sterile kind of in-fighting, to one that can create positive growth and change in your own relationships.

5
MOLLY & BRIAN
The Mask of False Humility

If there should ever have been founded a 'Guild of False Modesty', surely the strongest candidate for its first president must be that slimy character in Charles Dickens' *David Copperfield* – Uriah Heep.

Observing Uriah at work in Mr Wickfield's office, Master Copperfield enquired whether or not Mr Heep was a great lawyer. 'Me, Master Copperfield?' said Uriah. 'Oh, no! I'm a very umble person. I am aware that I am the umblest person going', said Uriah Heep, modestly; 'let the other be where he may.'[22]

In unforgettable imagery, Charles Dickens paints a literary portrait of this obsequious character who conceals his cunning and skullduggery behind an oily facade of false humility. Eventually, however, this villain is unmasked. David Copperfield says:

> Though I had long known that his servility was false, and
> all his pretences knavish and hollow, I had had no
> adequate conception of the extent of his hypocrisy, until I
> now saw him with his mask off. The suddenness with
> which he dropped it, when he perceived that it was useless
> to him; the malice, insolence, and hatred he revealed; the
> leer with which he exulted, even at this moment, in the evil
> he had done – all this time being desperate too, and at
> his wits' end for the means of getting the better of us –
> though perfectly consistent with the experience I had of
> him, at first took even me by surprise, who had known him
> so long, and disliked him so heartily.[23]

Uriah Heep must stand as the warning sign for all who profess to be 'the very umblest person going'.

I remember being confronted very strongly by some members of a group I was working with in Chicago concerning my own false humility. It was not, I trust, in Uriah's league, but it was nonetheless a rude awakening for me. I had asked a member of our group to accompany me on the viola while I played on the piano a minuet of J. S. Bach. I turned up with the music and I was asked how it went. Without hesitation, I gave a rendition of the tune by whistling it all the way through with accurate pitch. This led to gasps of astonishment and expressions of appreciation, which I proceeded at once to dismiss with a kind of 'oh-it's-nothing-really' response. I was unprepared for the way I was immediately confronted about my dismissive treatment of their appreciation, and I was reminded very forcefully that it was OK to recognise the gifts which I possessed and to accept their appreciation. (This mixture of confrontational love I was later to discover in David Augsburger's book, *Caring Enough to Confront*.[24]) I am grateful to that group for teaching me a lesson about false humility and for helping me towards a recognition and re-owning of my own gifts and accomplishments. In this process, I recalled the many occasions when praise had been restrained behind the 'we-mustn't-give-him-a-big-head' script. To be honest, praise and appreciation embarrassed me, but this loving confrontation allowed me to explore more deeply my own scripts of self-denial and self-depreciation. The *falsity* of my modesty lay in my own crying *need* for such recognition and affirmation while at the same time *denying that need*.

Where such scripts of false modesty are operating between couples they often create havoc. They do this by creating a *barrier* between people, which filters out truth and integrity, and places a high value on untruth and distortion.

Take Molly and Brian for instance. They are both teachers, and have been married for about five years. They have no children, choosing instead to further their respective careers and get themselves on a secure financial footing. They face the usual problems of a two-career family: work-allocation at their house and sharing in the family chores and house-keeping. A constant factor in the background of their relationship is Brian's sense of inferiority. While Molly has a first-class honours degree, Brian only managed a lower-second. He usually manages to hide his sense of resentment behind a mask of over-confidence. Molly tries to play down her own accomplishments for Brian's sake, and tries at every opportunity to reinforce his own strong points. She is therefore very self-effacing, and often dismisses the recognition which her gifts and talents bring her. However, she is now under pressure from her Head to apply for a headship at a local school. It is the next logical step for her to take in her career, but she hesitates fearing what effect this might have upon Brian who has recently been disappointed in his application for a Scale-3 post at his school. Molly feels trapped between pursuing her career which would give her more job-satisfaction and a higher income, and coping with Brian who might feel even more disadvantaged. She is tempted to delay her application for the headship but many of her colleagues are pressing her to apply.

She decides to approach Brian on the subject, to see how he feels about it.

MOLLY: I've been thinking about applying for the vacancy at Broadmead School . . .

BRIAN: Not the headship!

MOLLY: Yes, that's the one. Well, actually it was David [*her head*] that suggested it. He thinks I'm ready for a move and he's advised me strongly to apply. What do you think?

BRIAN: The headship? That's another ball-game! Are you sure you're ready?

MOLLY: Well, yes and no. It is about time I was thinking of a move, and I must admit I'm a bit excited about the challenge.

BRIAN: Challenge? Headache, more like. Just think of all that responsibility, the staff problems, managing to keep the peace with the Unions – who needs that?

MOLLY: But there's more to it than that, Brian. There's the money for one thing . . .

BRIAN: . . . and more tax to pay! Is it worth it?

MOLLY: You don't sound very keen on the idea.

BRIAN: You do what you like. I'm only pointing out the other side. Of course, you'll be home later, and leaving earlier. It'll mean more for me to do as well. Have you thought of that?

MOLLY: Perhaps I'd better forget the whole thing, then? I'll tell David in the morning I've decided not to apply. Maybe I'm not ready for a move after all.

By a close examination of this encounter we can discover more about what is going on under the surface.

Script	Analysis
M1 I've been thinking about applying for the vacancy at Broadmead School ...	
B1 Not the headship!	Brian does not allow Molly to finish what she has been thinking – his 'not' giving the game away regarding the suggestion.
M2 Yes, that's the one. Well, actually it was David that suggested it.	M attempts to deflect some of the responsibility for this suggestion onto her Head.
He thinks I'm ready for a move and he's advised me strongly to apply. What do you think?	M appears to be reluctant to state what *she* herself thinks.
B2 The headship? That's another ball-game!	Consciously or unconsciously, such a move (and the added status of a headship) will put further distance between the positions of M and B.
Are you sure you're ready?	Perhaps B is concealing his own statement behind this question: '*I* am not ready for you to make this move'.
M3 Well, yes and no. It is about time I was thinking of a move, and I must admit I'm a bit excited about the challenge.	M is hesitatingly stating her own attraction to the new possibility. She shares her feelings of excitement ...
B3 Challenge? Headache, more like.	... which B immediately squashes. His response is consistently negative (see B4).
Just think of all that responsibility, the staff problems, managing to keep the peace with the Unions – who needs that?	B points out all the negative aspects of the new job – but he does *not* reveal his own inner feelings.
M4 But there's more to it than that, Brian. There's the money for one thing ...	M reacts to B's negativity but again is interrupted ...

87

B4 ... and more tax to pay! Is it worth it?

... by a counter-charge of another negative kind. B is appealing to the doubt already existing in M's mind, although one of the real reasons for the doubt is what effect such a move will have upon B's ego.

M5 You don't sound very keen on the idea.

M at last confronts B with her awareness of his negative responses.

B5 You do what you like. I'm only pointing out the other side.

B does not respond to M's confrontation. Instead he deflects what he is truly feeling on to M and the decision she must make. He has not once affirmed the positive side of M's idea. His 'only' therefore is dishonest.

Of course, you'll be home later, and leaving earlier. It'll mean more for me to do as well. Have you thought of that?

B continues to explore the effects of such a move upon himself – no thought is given to M, only so far as her changing jobs will affect him. This is a legitimate *part* of the implications of such a change, but B treats it as the *whole*.

M6 Perhaps I'd better forget the whole thing, then? I'll tell David in the morning I've decided not to apply. Maybe I'm not ready for a move after all.

The cop-out! M surrenders to B's pressure, since she sees that B is not going to affirm her in her pursuit of this job. She rationalises this 'decision' under the guise of 'not ready', colluding with B's question in B2.

The final point of not being ready is a moot point: exactly who is not ready for this move? While Molly is prepared to see both the problems and the possibilities, Brian sees only the problems. Given that this is a typical instance of the way Molly and Brian relate we can draw some general conclusions about their relationship.

As a couple they appear to major on the exploration of the practicalities of change, but either underplay or ignore their feelings. Brian does not respond to Molly's feelings of excitement which the possibility of the new job activates within her. Brian conceals his own feelings behind a wall of negativity, but Molly allows Brian to get away with this. Molly therefore is not taking responsibility for what she is allowing Brian to do to her. Her one confrontation (M5) only leads to further implications (for Brian) if she takes the job, and a dismissal of her awareness of his lack of enthusiasm.

Insofar as this is a typical transaction between Molly and Brian, we must also note the playing down of Molly's pursuit of her career. There is no encouragement from Brian, no positive input, no sharing of her sense of excitement. What appears to be a challenge to her, turns out to be a headache for him. The fact that such a promotion would further the status-gap between them is never aired. This transaction is significant more by what it conceals than what it reveals underneath the façade of rationalisation.

Avoidance, therefore, seems to mark the way Molly and Brian relate. The writer Sam Keen[25] defines anxiety as A/void/dance, and this fairly typifies what is going on between Brian and Molly – *a void dance* around the real issues of status, feelings, and emotional reactions to new possibilities. This relationship appears to flourish on concealment rather than on revelation of who Molly and Brian truly are. Of course, we do not know what level of self-awareness each of these two people possesses, and how far they are truly conscious of what is going on between them. What is apparent, however, is the modesty which is hindering Molly from reaching her potential, choosing rather to play down her own professional worth for the sake of the uneasy truce which exists in her marriage.

Fear, therefore, is another element in this relationship. Molly and Brian do not appear to relate out of a loving trust in each other. Rather, Molly accedes to Brian's whining 'what-about-me' scripts and thereby avoids the showdown. The long-term implications of this style of relating includes the probability that Molly will always have to accede to Brian's wishes by adopting a pattern of self-denial. She must deny her needs for promotion and recognition in her career; she must deny her own potential as a human being in terms of her own self-fulfilment; she must deny her right, ultimately, to be her own person and to exercise her own autonomy. She will surrender these to Brian's needs not to be left too far behind Molly in their respective careers, and the sexist overtones of this behaviour pattern are quite obvious. Molly and Brian's marriage relationship is based, therefore, on Molly's willingness to make concessions. Such self-sacrifice might, in some eyes, appear laudable since the stability of the relationship is not threatened and the marital boat is not rocked. This will continue to be so until Molly comes to a fresh awareness of what she is doing.

Let us suppose, therefore, for the sake of illustration, that Molly does come to this new awareness. Let us suppose she decides not to be governed by what Brian wants, but by what she wants. What might happen if she gave up her false modesty concerning her potential, and really wanted to have a shot at getting the new job. How might the dialogue go? Perhaps something like this:

MOLLY: I've decided to have a shot at that job, Brian, after all. I put my application in today.

BRIAN: The last I heard, you said you didn't think you were ready for a move. What changed your mind?

MOLLY: I also said I was excited about the challenge of the new job, but you didn't appear to hear that!

BRIAN: But have you thought of the problems, the difficulties . . .

MOLLY: 'Problems' – 'difficulties' – that's all you appear to notice. When I talk about the extra money, all you hear is 'more tax'!

BRIAN: Why ask me what I think, then, if you've already made up your mind? You're not interested in my views.

MOLLY: I had not made up my mind when I first mentioned the subject. I wanted us to discuss all the pros and cons, but all I got from you were the cons! You hadn't a good word or a positive idea about the new job. You never once asked how I felt about it, nor whether this would be a good move for me. You only saw how this job might affect *you*!

BRIAN: That's not fair!

MOLLY: Nevertheless, it's true. I'm tired of trying to fit in with your ideas and wants. I've decided to think of my career for a change. I sit and listen night after night about your problems at school; do you ever think that I might not have had a good day? Do you ever ask what kind of a day I've had? No!

BRIAN: You never said . . .

MOLLY: Maybe not. But I'm saying it now. You seem incapable of thinking or caring about what might be good for me, and this job would be a good move for me. I'm sorry you can't appreciate that.

BRIAN: Am I that self-centred, then?

MOLLY: Frankly, yes! And I'm partly angry because I've never said so before now. I've not been honest with you about my true feelings in the past. I've been protecting you somehow, supporting you in your career while not getting much support from you about mine. It's always been a touchy subject between us and I often get the feeling that you're jealous in some way of my career. You're always making sneaky remarks to our friends, covered up in a joke, introducing me as 'my Deputy Head'.

BRIAN: Can't you take a joke, now, then?

MOLLY: My sense of humour is as alive as yours, but this is beyond a joke. You never stop to think what might lie behind these remarks of yours. It's obviously a subject which occupies a lot of your mind since you mention it so often.

BRIAN: So what are you asking?

MOLLY: I'm asking you to be proud of me and my work, and to think of it as just as worthwhile as your own. I know I've been guilty of playing my job down in the past, only to give you a boost, but this is simply dishonest. I'm sorry I deceived you by doing that.

BRIAN: So you never really cared, then?

MOLLY: Of course I cared. But I see now that I was caring for your job at the expense of my own. I was putting you first, and ignoring myself and what I really want. Well, I really want that headship and I'm going for it.

What is going on here? Molly has, apparently, stopped protecting Brian from how she feels and has taken responsibility for what she has been allowing Brian to do to her. She is honest about her anger and how part of it is with herself for what she has, previously, allowed to happen. Molly appears to have reached a decision regarding her own future, not in an 'either-or', 'you-*or*-me' pattern, but in a way that includes her own needs which issues in a 'both-and', 'you-*and*-me' pattern. Where one of the partners in a relationship is continuously putting themselves down, paying the price for the other's happiness and feelings of well-being, there is always the chance that, with new awareness, the backlash will come. This usually means a crisis in the relationship since the old way of relating is being replaced with a new, and thus unfamiliar, way of relating and new rules have to be worked through.

Molly and Brian represent those couples who operate out of a pattern whereby one partner chooses the role of the *peace-maker* at the expense of their own personal satisfaction and well-being. The wider connotation, of course, is seen in the general area of 'male-chauvinistic-piggery' whereby the career of the male is deemed (by him) to be of more importance than the career of his female counterpart. Very often, however, as we have seen in the case of Molly, the female *colludes* with such chauvinistic attitudes in the interests of peace and harmony. Yet, as we have seen, this merely provides a breeding-ground for deep discontent within Molly which is far more lethal to the relationship than her confrontation of Brian.

Perhaps Molly's confrontation, and her assertion of her own autonomy and self-worth, can provide Brian and her with a new foundation upon which to build a firmer relationship based on openness and integrity, rather than avoidance and self-denial. Molly dared to assert her true needs and feelings, and laid aside the mask of false modesty.

6
JANE & ROGER
The Weapon of Helplessness

One of the most common ingredients among the styles of arguing some couples adopt concerns the question of helplessness. As we observe and analyse some of these arguments, it becomes apparent that one of the partners is using helplessness as a weapon in a style of 'dirty fighting'.

Some psychologists[26] speak of the factor of 'learned' or 'acquired helplessness' which becomes an integral part of a person's personality. They mean that some of us have learned from an early age to believe that we are powerless in certain circumstances, and that there is nothing that we can do to help ourselves. Some of the experiences which lead us to this conclusion are, of course, based on solid fact. There are many situations which, as young children, we are not able to change. In our infantile stage of dependence and vulnerability many of us were faced with overwhelming odds which reinforced our sense of helplessness. The vindictive mother, the older sibling, the abuse from father or baby-sitter, all appeared too powerful for us to control or defeat. Thus our early experiences can lead to deep feelings of helplessness which are expressed in what Eric Berne called 'life scripts'. These might sound like, 'To be me, is to be helpless'; or, 'Others are more powerful than I am'; or, more simply, 'I can't cope'. When these scripts, arising out of genuine experiences very early in life, get submerged into our unconscious store of memories, they can go on acting within us to produce *a generalised attitude* towards ourselves and others. This is the dynamic which often surfaces within inter-personal relationships as a sense of 'acquired helplessness'.

What makes this sense of helplessness potentially dangerous in relationships is that we are importing an essentially *infantile* awareness into *adult* contexts. A response of helplessness to an overwhelming situation in our childhood might well have been appropriate; it is quite *in*appropriate to adopt the same, infantile, attitude towards situations we meet in adulthood. This attitude gets reinforced when we discover that *being helpless has its rewards*.

FIRST, it means we can escape taking responsibility. We leave decision-making to others, then they can take the blame for anything that goes wrong. 'Well, that was your decision, not mine!' is a fairly typical line in some couples' arguments.

SECOND, it means a high state of dependency on other people (since, of course, they have all the power!). This 'acquired helplessness' places a heavy burden on the other person. They must 'carry' the helpless partner emotionally, and often act as their rescuer, spokesman/spokeswoman, and defender. When the 'strong' partner is asked why they take on this burden, the answer is often, 'S/He's not up to it, you know'.

THIRD, it will mean an almost total abdication on the part of the 'strong' partner to the wishes of the 'weak' one. Here is the sinister result of this life script of acquired helplessness: *the helpless partner usually ends up totally controlling the other person.* The weak partner, in fact, has *all the power*.

These 'rewards' of helplessness (avoidance of responsibility, chronic dependency, and control of others) are necessary to bear in mind when wondering why people hang on to their 'life script' of helplessness. Too much is invested in it to give it up easily!

When these are operating within a close relationship, the possible outcome is clear. Let us illustrate this by a close look at Roger and Jane.

They have been married for four years. Roger is an only child, and Jane has five brothers and sisters. Roger works as an assistant manager in a small firm of jewellers, a position he has held for about seven years. Jane works as a nursing sister at the local general hospital. They have no children, and Jane often laughs about Roger being 'her baby'. Roger responds by praising Jane for 'doing everything for him' and he often tells his friends he wouldn't know what to do without her.

Recently, Jane has been feeling tired and over-worked. She has been trying to suppress feelings of anger towards Roger for not pulling his weight while at the same time feeling guilty about her anger. One evening Jane arrives home later than usual, having stayed on the ward to cover for a sick colleague. She finds Roger sitting in the lounge, watching TV.

JANE: Sorry I'm late. Had to cover for Rita who's off sick . . .

ROGER: She's not the only one! I've been waiting for my dinner for the past hour. I'm starving.

JANE: Why ever didn't you start cooking it, then?

ROGER: I didn't know what we were having, did I?

JANE: You could have looked in the 'fridge. The chops are there – and you could have peeled some potatoes in any case.

ROGER: But you know I'm not good at that sort of thing. I never know where you keep things.

JANE: Then would you please lay the table, while I get the meal.

ROGER: I'm just in the middle of *Eastenders* – I'll do it in a minute . . .

JANE: You were starving a moment ago!

(Jane goes into the kitchen to prepare and cook the meal. She comes into the lounge shortly afterwards to find Roger asleep in the chair . . . she erupts!)

JANE: Roger! You've not laid the table. I asked you to help.

ROGER: I'm tired.

JANE: And what do you think I am? I've been on my feet all day as well, you know.

ROGER: All right, all right, don't go on so. Where's the cloth?

JANE: Where it always is – in the sideboard drawer.

ROGER: Which drawer?

JANE: Why don't you just look – there's only two of them! You're about as useful as a sick headache!

ROGER: And whose fault is that, eh? You want to organise everything in this house, and then expect me to know where you've put things! You're not in the hospital ward now, you know!

JANE: And you're not in the nursery now, either!! It's about time you grew up, Roger. You're thirty-three, you know, not three.

ROGER: What's got into you?

JANE: I'll tell you what's got into me. I'm sick and tired of you treating this place like an hotel, and me as your chambermaid! I wait on you hand and foot. I do a full day's work, just like you, but I have to take the house on single-handed. Well, it can't go on like this any longer.

ROGER: You've never complained about this before.

JANE: I've tried to ignore it up until now, that's why, but now it's getting on top of me. I think it's time we changed the way things have been around here.

ROGER: I don't see why. Everything's been OK so far – why start changing things now?

JANE: You haven't heard a word I've said, have you? Everything is NOT fine, do you hear? I want you to start taking an equal share of the responsibility of running this house, for starters. This hasn't been a husband-and-wife partnership; it's been more like a nursery!

ROGER: So now you're criticising me for having let you run the house, are you? You've been the one wearing the trousers in this house. You make all the decisions. You know how dependent on you I am – we've always been this way.

JANE: Well, not any longer! I need a man around this house, not a child.

ROGER: It's you who's being childish! Just because you were late home . . .

JANE: That isn't the point! I get home late to find you like a helpless child sitting watching TV, and complaining about being starved! Now *that's* childish! Grow up, Roger, and start acting like a man.

ROGER: Right, then, I will (*puts coat on*) . . . If you want me, I'll be at Mum's. At least I'll get fed there!

This scenario illustrates two general points concerning couples arguing. *First*, it shows us the possibilities which are contained within a relational crisis. I understand that in the Chinese language, the two characters which make up their word for 'crisis' are 'danger' and 'opportunity'. In this interchange between Roger and Jane we can see both the *danger* of questioning the way in which their relationship has held together over their four years of marriage, and also the *opportunity* of changing things for the better. *Secondly*, this dialogue illustrates the way in which certain characteristics which worked *for* Roger and Jane at one stage of their relationship, may work *against* them at another stage. Their assumed script of 'You-be-mother – I'll-be-little-boy' suited them *both* for a while, until the stress and other consequences of this script began to cry out for a change in their behaviour pattern. Many couples find themselves in this situation somewhere along their journey, where what suited them both in the past now becomes a *block* to further growth in their relationship.

Now, in more detail, let us see what lies underneath Jane's confrontation of Roger:

Script	Analysis
J1 Sorry I'm late. Had to cover for Rita who's off sick ...	
R1 She's not the only one!	Sarcasm covering his anger.
I've been waiting for my dinner for the past hour. I'm starving.	There is no response to Jane's extra workload and no awareness shown of her needs. Roger is only aware of his own.
J2 Why ever didn't you start cooking it, then?	This, directed to R's 'waiting'. Doubtless, J's 'mothering-role' has reinforced this passivity throughout their marriage. Her pigeons are coming home to roost!
R2 I didn't know what we were having, did I?	Ignorance is a way of abandoning responsibility – a rather pathetic response!
J3 You could have looked in the 'fridge. The chops are there – and you could have peeled some potatoes in any case.	J is addressing R as an adult, not now as a child. This change of approach is not registered by R for some time.
R3 But you know I'm not good at that sort of thing. I never know where you keep things.	R still in the role of the little boy – whining at 'bad mother' for expecting too much of him!
J4 Then would you please lay the table, while I get the meal.	Ignoring R's whining, J makes an alternative approach to enlist R's assistance.
R4 I'm just in the middle of *Eastenders* – I'll do it in a minute ...	A total lack of appreciation of how J is feeling. His pleasure must come first. This is also a means of *controlling* J's attempt to get co-operation, and says, 'I'll do it in my time, not yours.'
J5 You were starving a moment ago!	

97

(*Exit to kitchen*)

J6	Roger! You've not laid the table. I asked you to help.	J maintains her insistence that R should help.
R6	I'm tired.	R wriggles to get out of such help. Rather than say how he feels about J's expectations, he avoids this behind a façade of tiredness.
J7	And what do you think I am?	J also conceals her feelings behind this response, not making the statement behind the question (see G2)
	I've been on my feet all day as well, you know.	J tries, indirectly (see G1) to convey her true feelings, but it goes unnoticed.
R7	All right, all right, don't go on so. Where's the cloth?	R wants to avoid J's needs, so changes tack to his well-used role of helpless child. He is really asking J here to rescue him.
J8	Where it always is – in the sideboard drawer.	J tries to get out of her rescuing role by addressing R as an adult.
R8	Which drawer?	A typically helpless response from R. He is trying to *manipulate* J into doing the task for him.
J9	Why don't you just look – there's only two of them! You're about as useful as a sick headache!	J's frustration issues in a verbal attack now, to which R responds . . .
R9	And whose fault is that, eh? You want to organise everything in this house, and then expect me to know where you've put things!	R now exposes one of the basic assumptions of their relationship: J is the organiser, the active one. R is now saying, in a cloaked way, that she can't have it both ways!
	You're not in the hospital ward now, you know!	Alluding to J's role at work, he now uses this in his verbal

counter-attack.

J10 And you're not in the nursery now, either!! It's about time you grew up, Roger. You're thirty-three, you know, not three.

Now J counter-attacks more fiercely. Underneath, of course, J knows that there is some truth in what R is saying. Since her relational role of 'mother' is challenged, she now responds by challenging his role as 'child'. The whole basis of their previous way of relating is now up for grabs.

R10 What's got into you?

He reflects the novelty of seeing J like this. By not responding to J10 R appears to be backing down first. He has more to lose.

J11 I'll tell you what's got into me. I'm sick and tired of you treating this place like an hotel, and me as your chamber-maid! I wait on you hand and foot. I do a full day's work, just like you, but I have to take the house on single-handed. Well, it can't go on like this any longer.

An obviously long-standing resentment now surfaces. The returns for nursing R are now no longer outweighing the disadvantages, and J is stating her case for a change in their previously accepted way of running their lives.

R11 You've never complained about this before.

This statement means: 'You are unilaterally changing the whole basis of our relationship!'

J12 I've tried to ignore it up until now, that's why, but now it's getting on top of me. I think it's time we changed the way things have been around here.

J confesses she has not been honest about her resentment. Trying to ignore problems only makes them bigger. She now makes her bid for a change in how they relate.

R12 I don't see why. Everything's been OK so far – why start changing things now?

He does not hear J's expression of stress – he only responds to his own inner fears of how change will affect *him*.

J13 You haven't heard a word I've said, have you? Everything's NOT fine, do you hear? I want you to start taking an equal

J gallantly confronts R's lack of awareness and sympathy to her statement in J12. J clearly spells out what she wants.

share of the responsibility of running this house, for starters.

This hasn't been a husband-and-wife partnership; it's been more like a nursery! | J gives an explicit statement of how she perceives the relationship – one in which she, of course, has been hitherto happily colluding.

R13 So now you're criticising me for having let you run the house, are you? | Unaware of how *he* has previously benefited from the old way of relating, he questions J's right to criticise him for something she wanted in the first place.

You've been the one wearing the trousers in this house. | Decoded, this means: 'I'm the one who has allowed you to wear the trousers . . .' Blaming statements like these usually rebound upon the perpetrator!

You make all the decisions. | = 'I have allowed you to make all the decisions.'

You know how dependent on you I am – we've always been this way. | R and J have related out of *dependency needs*: R's to be looked after, and J's to be needed.

J14 Well, not any longer! I need a man around this house, not a child. | J now spells out what the new agenda, based on her adult (not parenting) needs, will look like. She is relinquishing her role as nursemaid/mother. She finally acknowledges she needs a man.

R14 It's you who's being childish! Just because you were late home . . . | A weak counter-accusation, clutching at straws to prevent such a dramatic change that threatens to overwhelm R.

J15 That isn't the point! I get home late to find you like a helpless child sitting watching TV, and complaining about being starved! Now *that's* childish! Grow up, Roger, and start acting like a man. | J brushes aside R's attempt to engender guilt, by a clear and unambiguous statement about R's chronic helplessness.

R15 Right, then, I will. If you want me, I'll be at Mum's. At least I'll get fed there!

R's only way of 'acting like a man' is to leave! He goes home to *mother* – and J's attempt (at least for now) to get Roger to take some adult responsibility has failed.

The above scenario is fairly typical of the relationship which some couples adopt. It is based on the 'pay-off' principle, whereby each partner gains something they need from their behaviour pattern. The basis of this pattern might be 'sick' (that is, neither Jane's need to 'mother' nor Roger's need to be 'mothered' was ever spelt out explicitly); nevertheless, there was enough return from this way of relating to keep it going. Like other 'sick' scripts, they keep going until one of the partners discovers that the pay-off is being ouweighed by the disadvantages. In this case, it was Jane. In order to *gain* an adult relationship with Roger she had to *lose* her mothering role. As we saw, Roger appeared to have far more invested in the agenda of this marriage than Jane did, so he sought temporary satisfaction of his 'child' needs by going back to his real mother.

The difficulty of changing a 'sick' relationship like Jane and Roger's is that the *original understanding* of their way of relating had to be exposed. It is this risk which makes many couples stick with the script they have! Guilt (at changing the script) and anger (at not changing it) vie with each other in turn.[27] Either the frustrated partner will swallow hard and go back to their old (blocked) way of relating, or they will bite the bullet and opt for change and growth in their relationship. Of course, there are no guarantees. For some couples, such a traumatic change will lead to an end of the relationship when one partner finds the journey to a more mature and adult style of behaviour too threatening. But changing the scripts of a relationship, like Roger and Jane, is far from impossible. They may need professional help to do so* but the will to work towards a more adult form of relating must be present if this help is to be effective.

* A list of professional agencies will be found on page 132.

7
JOHN & PAT
The Protection Racket

The original 'protection racket' was, I believe, started in the United States. Mobsters like Al Capone and John Dillenger had gangs that used to intimidate local shopkeepers and dance-hall proprietors in the 1930s by demanding 'protection money', a kind of 'insurance' against having their shops smashed up or otherwise put out of business. This means of extortion was widespread, and many local businessmen paid up as the price of peace and quiet.

Something like this is to be seen operating within some personal relationships. Partners are often engaged in the protection of one another, and on occasions this can be very supportive and positive. For example, any protection from physical attack or verbal abuse can be entirely appropriate. But there is another, inappropriate means of using protection which needs further examination.

Sometimes when I am counselling one of the partners of a marriage, a stream of resentments and misgivings will pour out from the long history of their relationship. One of my usual responses to such disclosures runs something like this: 'Have you told your husband (wife, partner, etc.) how you feel about what they are doing?' My question is almost always answered by, 'Oh no! I daren't!' Or, 'Oh! I couldn't do that, it would shatter him!' Their silence is the 'protection money' they are paying for the sake of peace and quiet. Instead of honest confrontation of the partner, a wall of silent suffering is built up which ensures that the resentment and pain is never disclosed. Rather than see their partner 'shattered', they will grin and bear it. Yet, behind the sickening grin lies real pain. Even when this is finally disclosed to a friend or a counsellor as a last desperate act to find a solution, they are very often assailed by a deep sense of guilt and disloyalty.

What lies behind this mode of behaviour? FIRST, the person who does the complaining is actually protecting himself. His silence is the price he pays for not having to confront his partner with his anger, pain or resentment. If what he wishes to complain of should have the effect of hurting his partner or causing tears (or another form of emotional reaction) then he would far rather keep quiet and go on suffering in silence and putting up with it. SECOND, the whole basis of the relationship is now transferred to one of deceit and half-truth. The aggrieved partner must learn to say 'Yes', when he means 'No'; to say 'I'm fine', when he is not fine; to say 'No, nothing's wrong', when everything is wrong. THIRD, their silence ensures that their partner lives in a kind of 'cloud-cuckoo-land', far away from the painful realities of the aggrieved partner's feelings. Unaware of such feelings, they are denied the opportunity of working towards some improvement since their partner is keeping them in the dark. FOURTH, the fear of a partner being 'shattered' by the truth is often a kind of projection. As we saw (p. 7), this is a means of defending ourselves by projecting on to others fantasies or feelings which we cannot cope with ourselves. Very often, what shatters a partner is not the truth, but the fact of its *concealment* over a long period of time. FIFTH, it is a surrender of one's power. By this I mean that by remaining silent in the face of behaviour which is causing you unhappiness and pain you are adding to the power and control the other person has over you (see further, chapter 8). As we noticed in Guideline 12, you are not taking responsibility for what you are allowing the other person to do to you. In refusing to use your right of confrontation you are enhancing the power of your partner over you. You are reinforcing his or her power to spoil your life and you are also reinforcing your own feelings of weakness and despair. You then opt for the role of victim within the relationship.

These five consequences of the 'protection racket' are often brought to light within a marital or couple's counselling session. For the sake of illustration let us take the situation that John and Pat find themselves in.

John and Pat have lived together for about three years and have known each other from school days. Pat was never short of boy-friends, being dark, petite and very attractive, but no relationship seemed to last very long. John somehow seemed different from her other boy-friends, quieter and more understanding. Pat's parents had split up during her late teens and by her early twenties her mother had remarried. Pat did not get along well with her stepfather and had been thinking of leaving home for some time, when things began to get a bit more serious with John. At her suggestion, and with increasing insistence, she and John moved into a flat together about three years ago. At first things went well. Her general moodiness seemed to improve and she was pleased with John's easy-going manner and the way he appeared to fit in with whatever she wanted.

John was very much in love with Pat but was far from sure either of them was ready for marriage. The suggestion of moving in together seemed a good compromise. John was well aware of Pat's moodiness at times, but she usually dismissed the importance of this by saying it was 'the wrong time of the month'. Pat also seemed to begrudge John any time he spent on his own, either on his studies for his accountancy examinations or his weekly evening at the squash courts. He always noticed a chill in the air when he got home from the Leisure Centre and how Pat's headaches seemed to coincide exactly with those evenings he spent out. Nothing would be said, but there was usually the unmistakable air of disapproval surrounding Pat, making it hard for John to make contact with her. At these times John would make an extra effort to cheer her up until things were right again. Now and then John would become aware that the relationship seemed to be getting a bit one-sided, and that he was doing all the giving. But he soon pushed such thoughts away to the back of his mind, reassuring himself that Pat really did love him; she just had some 'funny ways', that was all.

However, things began to go from bad to worse during the period leading up to John's examinations. Pat began to resent his studying in the evening, and appeared to be more demanding than ever on his time. She would go into long periods of silence and would refuse to discuss what was wrong. John felt more and more rejected but managed to put on a brave face for Pat's benefit. He started to worry about his examinations and to have doubts of his success in spite of his working hard. He worked harder with Pat to bring her round but he found the effort unrewarding and it resulted in him being more tired than ever.

Finally, he poured all this story out to a friend of his at the Leisure Centre. The depth and scope of his misgivings surprised even John. He finally had to admit that he had avoided a confrontation of Pat's behaviour pattern for too long, and that things could not go on as they were. But – could he feel comfortable about hurting Pat with the truth of his feelings? He felt stuck between his *anger* at her childish behaviour and wanting to tell her so, and his *guilt* at doing anything to add to the problems she was already carrying. It seemed to John a 'no-win' situation. Since something had to be done, he finally decided to tell Pat about the conversation with his friend and trust to luck it would be all right in the end.

John arrived home from the Centre to find Pat in bed, reading. After his shower, John starts to talk to Pat:

JOHN: I need to talk to you, Pat.

PAT: There's nothing to talk about.

JOHN: I need to talk to you about us – about how things have been between us lately.

PAT: There's no point.

JOHN: I think our relationship has a point, and I'm trying to reach you in order that we can . . .

PAT: Reach me? You seem to have been busy doing just the opposite lately, what with your studying and going out with your mates.

JOHN: Look, Pat, I'm not finding this easy, you know. I'm trying to get through to you and all you're doing is building up the wall between us.

PAT: It's not me who's doing all the building, you know. You're just mean and ungrateful. I can't seem to get anything right with you. How dare you imply it's all my fault!

JOHN: Do you mind listening for a change? I'm not implying it's all your fault – I just want things to be different, that's all.

PAT: If you're not satisfied, you know what you can do, don't you?

JOHN: Satisfied? You must be joking! Do you know what I've had to put up with from you these past few months? Silence, moodiness, sulking, being frozen out – you've handed out the lot. Meanwhile, I've been giving and giving, and now I've nothing left to give. I'm empty.

PAT: You ungrateful sod!

JOHN: What have I to be grateful for? I've had to earn the crumbs of comfort you've been giving me lately! And I've paid dearly, I can tell you.

PAT: (*clearly shaken, and near to tears*) I don't know what's come over you . . .

JOHN: Let me enlighten you, then. I've bitten my tongue over these past few months so much it's almost fallen off! Well, now I'm saying what I should have said months ago.

PAT: What stopped you?

JOHN: To be honest, I didn't want to hurt you. I've been shielding you from my feelings of anger and resentment and I now know this isn't right. I care deeply for you and for our relationship but I also need you to know what I'm feeling.

PAT: And what about *my* feelings, then; don't they count?

JOHN: Of course they do. But I need you to tell me what they are instead of bottling them up inside you all the time. I'm just as guilty about that as you are.

PAT: I'm afraid that if I tell you what I'm feeling, you won't want me any more.

JOHN: Look, Pat, there's something special between us. We'd never have stayed together as long as we have done if there wasn't. Let's just trust each other with what we want to say and what we want to change and see where we go from there.

PAT: OK – I'll try and risk it if you will.

Well, John finally plucked up courage to tell Pat what had been going round his head for a few months, and somehow they found a way through the immediate confrontation to a place where they were prepared to take a risk by being honest and open with one another. It could have gone the other way. Pat could have clammed up and frozen John out, so let us see why this didn't happen as we look at this dialogue in further detail.

	Script	*Analysis*
J1	I need to talk to you, Pat.	A clear and direct expression of a need.
P1	There's nothing to talk about.	Pat does not hear John's need hence there is no response to it. P puts up her fence.
J2	I need to talk to you about us – about how things have been between us lately.	J repeats his need ... and states the agenda relating to that need. Wherever this argument is going at least it begins neutrally.

P2 There's no point.	Again P puts up her blanket of negativity, denying that talking has any validity.
J3 I think our relationship has a point, and I'm trying to reach you in order that we can ...	J refuses to get waylaid into the subject of whether or not there is a 'point' – he just assumes there is and focuses the 'point' upon their strained relationship – but he gets cut off ...
P3 Reach me? You seem to have been busy doing just the opposite lately, what with your studying and going out with your mates.	Taking no responsibility for how she has made 'reaching her' more difficult by *her* self-made barriers, she gets into a blaming frame of reference. She makes a 'you' statement instead of the 'I' statement which lies hidden beneath, something like 'I feel neglected'.
J4 Look, Pat, I'm not finding this easy, you know. I'm trying to get through to you and all you're doing is building up the wall between us.	J confesses to the difficulty he is experiencing in his attempt to get through P's defensive behaviour.
P4 It's not me who's doing all the building, you know. You're just mean and ungrateful. I can't seem to get anything right with you. How dare you imply it's all my fault!	P still refuses to accept *any* responsibility for what has happened, partly because J has never before confronted her like this.
J5 Do you mind listening for a change? I'm not implying it's all your fault – I just want things to be different, that's all.	J makes a clear request to be heard, since hardly any of P's responses are directly related to what J is saying.
P5 If you're not satisfied, you know what you can do, don't you?	J's attempt (J5) fails. He gets a 'take it or leave it' option. But this does have the effect of making J more open ...
J6 Satisfied? You must be joking! Do you know what I've had to put up with from you these past	J decides to stop protecting P from what he has been feeling. (For 'had to', read 'chose to'!)

107

few months? Silence, moodiness, sulking, being frozen out – you've handed out the lot. Meanwhile, I've been giving and giving, and now I've nothing left to give. I'm empty.

J catalogues the behaviour he has hitherto chosen to tolerate. He now makes an alternative choice, to *confront* rather than *collude*.

P6   You ungrateful sod!

P is stung by J6.

J7   What have I to be grateful for? I've had to earn the crumbs of comfort you've been giving me lately! And I've paid dearly, I can tell you.

J sees P's contributions as disproportionate to his own. He refuses to be grateful for what he has paid for.

P7   I don't know what's come over you . . .

P is now back on the defensive. She makes no attempt to challenge the truth of what J is saying. She changes tack, as a manoeuvre, to attribute this confrontation to some change in J.

J8   Let me enlighten you, then. I've bitten my tongue over these past few months so much it's almost fallen off! Well, now I'm saying what I should have said months ago.

P was right (in P7) but not in the way she thought. The change is in the decision to stop protecting P from the way J feels. J concedes his fault in not levelling with P before now.

P8   What stopped you?

A risky question, but the first inkling that P has shown that she is now listening to J.

J9   To be honest, I didn't want to hurt you. I've been shielding you from my feelings of anger and resentment and I now know this isn't right. I care deeply for you and for our relationship but I also need you to know what I'm feeling.

This is an important admission. J's statement is an ideal illustration of how care *and* confrontation can come together. He is fighting *for* the relationship, and uses open honesty as a 'clean' weapon.

P9   And what about *my* feelings, then? Don't they count?

P gets locked in again to 'what's in-it-for-me'. She is not hearing the concern in J9 for the relationship.

J10 Of course they do. But I need you to tell me what they are instead of bottling them up inside you all the time. I'm just as guilty about that as you are.

P is reassured that her feelings count, and J is inviting a full expression of them. He admits his own guilt for his past concealment.

P10 I'm afraid that if I tell you what I'm feeling, you won't want me any more.

The first hole in the wall! P lets some of what she is feeling come out: fear.

J11 Look, Pat, there's something special between us. We'd never have stayed together as long as we have done if there wasn't. Let's just trust each other with what we want to say and what we want to change and see where we go from there.

J reassures P by stating the 'specialness' of what they have. He invites a different style of relating based on trust and hope for their future.

P11 OK – I'll try and risk it if you will.

Aware of the dangers of this new style of relating, P agrees to a mutual risk-taking as they level with each other.

This interchange between John and Pat shows the difficulties of changing from a 'protection' style of relating to one based on an honest expression of feelings hitherto suppressed. John had to face Pat with the five consequences of a relationship based on the 'protection racket' style. *First*, he had to stop protecting *himself* from his anticipated response from Pat. He chose to expose himself to her pain and hurt. *Second*, he tried to re-establish the relationship on a basis of truth rather than concealment. He stopped the 'let's-pretend' game. *Third*, by letting Pat into his own misgivings and resentments (see J6) he allowed her the freedom to respond creatively to them. *Fourth*, by John's disclosures Pat might have been shaken, but she was not shattered. Initially she was taken by surprise when John decided to confront her wall of evasion, but eventually she was able to risk further exploration of ways in which they could improve their relationship. *Finally*, John gave up surrendering his power to Pat, and discovered that he did not need to go on behaving as a helpless victim.

The 'protection racket' demands a high price from those who play this couples game. John discovered new resources within himself *and within Pat* which could be used towards the enrichment of their life together. The energy used in the *concealment* of our pain is not available for the building up of relationships; hence, little building gets done. There is a scene in the film *Ordinary People* which illustrates this point.

The plot of the film concerns a family with two sons, the elder of which gets drowned in a boating accident. This precipitates a major crisis within the family, and the mother withdraws into a depression. The younger son is blamed by the mother and gets rejected by her. The understanding is that she had rather the younger son had died instead of the older. Eventually, the younger son seeks therapy in order to integrate this painful experience into his life. The therapist asks the son, 'Don't you ever get angry?' The son replies, 'I haven't the energy to get angry!' 'Do you realise,' asks the therapist, 'just how much energy you use up *not* getting angry?'

By repressing our legitimate feelings, therefore, we deny to ourself and to others the energy needed to improve relationships and our communication skills. John and Pat at least illustrate a more constructive way forward.

8
SIMON & KAREN
The Power Game

Each of the preceding dialogues included an important element in the arguing styles of the various couples, namely, power or dominance. It is time to bring this aspect out into the open in order to understand its importance and influence in human relationships.

In the case of Peter and Susan, the context of power concerned that of money and the control of expenditure on telephone bills. With Steve and Paula, Mike and Brenda, we noticed the issues of control over work-patterns and extra-marital activities which rob the relationship of vital resources without which their intimacy will starve and decline. With Molly and Brian it seemed to be the case that Brian's negativity was controlling Molly's advancement in her career, a power game in which, of course, Molly herself was at first happy to collude. Jane and Roger show us the power wielded by helplessness. In the argument between John and Pat we saw how the concealment of the truth from Pat was a surrender of John's power to her. When he finally gave up this behaviour pattern, he discovered he did not have to go on behaving like a helpless victim of Pat's whims.

Most couples start out with the ideal of 'partnership' rather than 'power' as the basis of their relationship. Where then, does this feature of power come from? Why is the need to dominate so inbred within most of us? And why do some of us resort to submission to the wishes of other people so readily?

During the course of our growth and development, we pick up the patterns of our family environment, and this is usually the first place where lessons about power and submission are learnt. We observe just who is in charge, and who wears the trousers in our household. We begin to understand that naked power and aggression can terrify us, and so 'toeing-the-line' becomes paramount, if we are to survive childhood. Later on, we discover that there is another kind of power, equally effective but ever so subtle. We observe the power and dominance that can be wielded by passivity, what the psychologists call the 'passive–aggressive personality'. Like Roger, in chapter 6, the seemingly helpless partner actually has all the power, but it is hidden behind a passive façade. We also discover that it actually feels better to be a winner than a loser, to get what we want rather than to feel deprived. So we learn the subtle tricks of how to get our own way when we don't happen to have much power in our family grouping. We resort to sulking, a passive–aggressive withdrawal stance; to whining, in order to wear down the will of the adult who is unwilling to meet our demands; to becoming a 'pleaser', over anxious to co-operate with others in order to win their approval and to place us in their 'good books'.

Every parent knows how their children try to 'get their own way' and what means they use. However co-operative parents might be, there will be times when a firm 'No' has to be said. Generally speaking, these 'No's constitute the very necessary boundaries that children need in order to feel secure within them, even though they will often kick and scream at them. Provided that their basic needs are being met within those boundaries (love, touch, adequate resources of food and a sense of general well-being), parental 'No's need not be harmful. Problems can occur later on if these boundaries are either too rigid and small, or too large and undefined, or if what was 'No' yesterday becomes 'Yes' today, producing a sense of utter confusion when the boundaries are changed almost on a day-to-day basis.

It is out of this childhood milieu that we bring into our adult life the lessons we have learnt about submission and dominance, about what brings the results we want and what does not, about how we win and how we lose. For most of us, these 'scripts' remain out of our awareness and our behaviour patterns are simply taken for granted. It is, however, potentially (and often actually) dangerous to import patterns of behaviour into our *adult* life which were more appropriate to an earlier stage of our development. For example, sulking in an adult is usually described as childish and rightly so. Such behaviour is simply regressing to a past pattern of behaviour which might have been the only 'weapon' we possessed as a child, but as adults we have a wider range of responses open to us. We simply have to give ourselves permission to use them. By speaking out, confronting, arguing, asserting ourselves we can bring an adult resolution to the problems we face without going back to infantile behaviour.

We see this issue clearly demonstrated in the relationship between Simon and Karen. He works as a motor mechanic at a local garage which his uncle owns. She used to work at the supermarket in town before she had their only child, Richard. The baby is now two years old. With the loss of Karen's wages the financial situation changed quite drastically. Their hopes of a house of their own had to be postponed, and they moved into a council flat on a large estate. They had been talking of Karen going back to work, but the cost of baby-minding would have taken up most of what Karen could have earned and they have shelved this idea for the present. They are still in the process of becoming a couple and have been plunged into parenthood earlier on in their relationship than they had planned. At the back of Simon's mind is the nagging resentment that Karen isn't working ('God knows, we need the money'), and at the back of Karen's mind is the feeling of resentment that Simon isn't pulling his weight with Richard ('If only he would realise how tired I get'). Such thoughts are never aired between them but they provide the hidden agenda against which the relationship is being carried on. The following is a fairly typical conversation after Simon gets home:

KAREN: Oh, Simon, do take those oily boots off in the hall. I've told you times.

SIMON: Can't I sit down first? Blimey, I've only just come in from work and you're on at me already.

KAREN: By the time you've sat down, you've got oil and grease all over the carpet where Richard plays. Take them off before you sit down.

SIMON: (*puts his boots in the hall, resentfully*) What's for tea?

KAREN: Sausage, egg and chips. I'm just going round the corner to get the peas; I forgot while I was out this afternoon. Keep an eye on the meal, will you. Oh, by the way, if Richard wakes up, his dummy's on the side.

SIMON: Oh hell! That's all I need.

(*Karen goes out. Richard starts to cry and while Simon attends to him, the sausages burn in the frying pan. Karen returns to a screaming child and a smoke-filled kitchen!*)

KAREN: What on earth is going on? Can't you do a simple thing like watching sausages?

SIMON: (*carrying Richard*) I can't be in two places at once, can I? If the meal had been ready in the first place this would never have happened.

KAREN: Ah, poor thing! How do you think I manage then all day – it's not all *Postman Pat* and *Playschool* you know. I leave you alone for five minutes and I come back to this mess.

SIMON: A fine home-coming this is! No food, a screaming child and a nagging wife – what more could I want?

KAREN: Instead of standing there feeling sorry for yourself, why don't you take Richard back to bed and make yourself useful.

SIMON: Can't you take him?

KAREN: Sure. But you find something else to eat. Like the man said, I can't be in two places at once!

In this domestic skirmish there is plenty of cut and thrust and, of the two, Karen appears to come out of it ahead on points. Amid the sounds of Richard crying and the smell of burnt sausages, another reality emerges: the power game. Let's analyse this dialogue and find out how the issue comes out in this rather ordinary domestic situation.

Script	*Analysis*
K1 Oh, Simon, do take those oily boots off in the hall. I've told you times.	Beneath this reasonable complaint in the interests of cleanliness, is another issue: getting Simon to do as he is told!
S1 Can't I sit down first?	The first of quite a few whining responses from S – an indirect means of communication cloaked in a question.
Blimey, I've only just come in from work and you're on at me already.	S experiences Karen as 'nagging' and K experiences S as 'whining'. Both are veiling deeper feelings.
K2 By the time you've sat down, you've got oil and grease all	Behind this other reasonable statement the issue of training

over the carpet where Richard plays.

S is lurking. K sneakily brings Richard in at this point on her side. Her request could stand on its own merit but she needs to reinforce this by using the baby.

Take them off before you sit down.

S2 What's for tea?

S does as he is told – a parent-child interaction.

K3 Sausage, egg and chips. I'm just going round the corner to get the peas; I forgot while I was out this afternoon. Keep an eye on the meal, will you? Oh, by the way, if Richard wakes up, his dummy's on the side.

It is tempting to find in this one of those things that gets 'forgotten' (see Guideline 9, p. 30ff) when emotions are not directly expressed.

S is now set up by K, by manipulating him into taking control of kitchen and child.

S3 Oh, hell! That's all I need.

A whine, to himself presumably. We do not know what his feelings are here; he merely uses sarcasm as a shield against them.

(*K goes out; and returns*)

K4 What on earth is going on? Can't you do a simple thing like watching sausages?

One way of gaining power for oneself is to 'deskill' the other person. This question is designed to reinforce in S his feelings of incompetence and inadequacy. K is sneering at S's inability to do a simple thing!

S4 I can't be in two places at once, can I? If the meal had been ready in the first place this would never have happened.

No sense of his responsibility here, since presumably he had never taken looking after Richard and the sausages as his real responsibility. He sees them as belonging to K, and reverses this to become 'all her fault'.

K5 Ah, poor thing!

Mockery and sarcasm,

concealing deeper feelings of anger.

How do you think I manage then all day – it's not all *Postman Pat* and *Playschool* you know.

Maybe S did *not* know how things were, since perhaps K had not told him before. Old resentments are coming out here, hitherto ignored.

I leave you alone for five minutes and I come back to this mess.

Parent-sounding scolding from K. The unspoken message is clear: 'I put you in control and see how you mess things up – better leave controlling this household to me!'

S5 A fine home-coming this is! No food, a screaming child and a nagging wife – what more could I want?

S returns K's use of mockery and sarcasm. Maybe there are *two* screaming children in the house?

K6 Instead of standing there feeling sorry for yourself, why don't you take Richard back to bed and make yourself useful?

K pours scorn on S's feelings which she correctly interpreted but which S did not convey directly. K can obviously 'read' S's veiled and indirect statements. She shows no sympathy for the way he feels. When his feelings are revealed, however indirectly, they are mocked.

S6 Can't you take him?

Having deskilled S, that is, having stripped him of any feelings of competence, S is reluctant to place himself in a vulnerable position. He tries to get K to take responsibility – but this misfires . . .

K7 Sure. But you find something else to eat. Like the man said, I can't be in two places at once!

. . . since K then gives him the task of finding and preparing the meal instead! By quoting back to him his words in S4, S is left disarmed, speechless and feeling humiliated.

Karen shows herself to be an expert in the art of systematic devaluation of Simon. Power and control are never mentioned, but that is surely the hidden agenda beneath this personal encounter. Karen is conveying a strong message to Simon about her need to be in charge of the relationship. He responds to this (hidden) message by whining, moaning, complaining and avoiding any full-frontal argument. Karen then reinforces both her own power and Simon's powerlessness by a process of deskilling her husband. She does this with consummate skill, reinforcing his incompetence and by systematically devaluing him. She then pours scorn on top of this ('Ah, poor thing!') and finally catches him in a trap of his own making by placing him in a no-win situation: he either puts the baby to bed or he cooks the meal. He wishes to do neither, but he is hoist with his own petard since Karen can't be in two places at once any more than he can.

What Karen does not appear to realise is that by this process of ridicule it is going to be harder for Simon to respond practically to her demands, even if those demands are reasonable in terms of sharing the household chores and parenthood. She is, unknowingly, reinforcing his childish sense of inferiority and thus making it less likely that she will gain any co-operation from him in the future. So she will then almost surely try to make stronger and stronger criticisms of him, and so the spiral will go down and down until something snaps.

This scenario is a variant of what we saw happening in chapter 6 ('The Weapon of Helplessness'), whereby Karen is actually creating this sense within Simon. What could the pay-off possibly be for Karen by maintaining this pattern of behaviour?

☐ FIRST, it makes quite sure that Simon's hidden agenda of resentment about her not working is kept buried and unspoken. By reminding him of her ability to cope and of his inability to cope, she is firmly establishing herself in a position of strength and dominance. 'You need me, you see!' is the unspoken message. The relationship would therefore be based on a 'one-up, one-down' arrangement, a parent-child game.

☐ SECOND, by presenting Simon with a continuous catalogue of his own shortcomings, she does not have to face her own. Simon's characteristic response is to moan and whine in a childish way to her demands, and try to wriggle out of them as best he can: 'Can't you do it?' So the question of just what was Karen doing on that evening, by 'forgetting' the peas, remains unasked. Did she (knowingly or unknowingly) set Simon up, so that he either had to take charge of the meal or remain without some part it? (This is a variation of the 'two-tie' game. The wife buys two ties for her husband. He comes down wearing the blue one and gets challenged with, 'What's wrong with the red one?') He can't win either way.

☐ THIRD, the way Karen is playing this particular version of 'the power game' means that the name of the game is never mentioned. If you reread the dialogue you will not find the words 'power', 'dominance', 'strength', 'weakness', mentioned at all. And yet, that is what the scenario is about. Should Simon challenge Karen with the question, 'Who put you in charge of this relationship?' or, 'You're trying to dominate me!' Karen could reply with the disarmingly innocent statement, 'I'm not trying to dominate you; it's just that you seem so incompetent to do the simplest of things!'

Of course, there is another side to 'the power game'. That is, the benefits to *Simon* which occur when Karen is in charge or control of the relationship. Some couples actually thrive on this kind of arrangement because there are benefits to *both* parties. Simon is playing the part of the *responder* in the marriage; he doesn't have to initiate anything. The Simons of this world allow (and actually prefer) their wives to take charge. In the music-hall version of the 'henpecked husband' all the sympathy usually goes to him, not his wife. He will be the object of pity. What is often not seen or appreciated is that such husbands sometimes play-act the 'hard-done-by' role, in order to elicit such sympathy. They take no responsibility for what they allow their wives to do to them. When confronted with my question, 'Why do you allow your wife to wear the trousers in your house?' most of my clients reply that I do not know their wives! Thus, the truth often turns out that the Simons of this world collude in this power game. (The Latin word, *colludere*, means 'to act in secret concert with; to play into one another's hands; to conspire; to play false; to act in play merely', *Oxford English Dictionary*.) All the benefits of helplessness (see chapter 6) are then available to the 'henpecked husband', and the last laugh will probably be on Karen.

Simon and Karen have not yet learnt the art of direct and open communication. Perhaps they are still too embarrassed or unsure of themselves to say what it is they are feeling. Karen could share her sense of tiredness with Simon, and he could share with Karen his wish that she find a job and so ease the financial burden on him as breadwinner. Neither of them seemed to show any appreciation of how the other partner was feeling. Neither of them was greeted with, 'How did your day go?' followed by a willingness to actually listen to the reply. Karen showed no empathy or under-standing of how Simon would feel after his day's work, and Simon showed no understanding of how Karen must feel after having Richard all day.

If this relationship is to grow and mature they need to find a new way of relating. At present, it is on its way to polarisation: 'persecutor/victim,' or 'top-dog/under-dog'. Should that take place, it would be a long and hard journey back to the middle. Before the stakes grow too high, they could experiment with a new agree-ment to be more honest and open with each other. The Guidelines offer a constructive way forward for Simon and Karen, and others.

Conclusion

As I begin to wrestle with the task of gathering up the fragments of this book and to make some tentative conclusions, I am reminded of the words of a writer to whom I owe a great deal: 'It is tempting to end neatly, to tie the loose ends, to sum up the tale and add an appropriate moral. But nothing living is tidy.'[28] Sam Keen is right, and I must learn to leave some things untidy. And there is nothing untidier than the world of human relationships.

I am aware that, for some of you at least, this book might have raised more issues than solutions. If this is so, it would have served its purpose. Not that my aim has been to mystify and confuse: quite the reverse. Indeed, I have kept before me the specific purpose of attempting to *demystify* the world of human relatedness and communication, the secrets of which are often believed to be in the hands of a few trained and experienced counsellors, psychologists and psychotherapists. I want such secrets as do exist to be made more readily available to the widest possible audience. I value the insights of the writer and psychotherapist, Sheldon Kopp, especially when he writes:

> . . . some Christians have opened their Bible to verses picked at random in hope of getting specific advice about how to solve problems. So, too, the psychotherapy patient may begin by trying to get the therapist to tell him what he is to do to be happy and how he is to live *without being fully responsible for his own life.*[29]

So should this book have raised more questions than answers, it is because I believe that our headlong search for the (usually instant) *solution* can blind us to the need to ask, as a necessary prerequisite, 'Yes, but what is the *problem?*' People are often looking for answers when, in my opinion, they should be concentrating more on ascertaining what the real questions are. I am asked almost every day to supply answers for people in pain and distress who come into my consulting room. I have no doubt that I must disappoint many of them when I refuse to supply 'off-the-peg' answers to questions that remain undefined.

I have made some attempt to unmask the issues which lie beneath some of the arguments outlined in the second part of this book. For instance, underlying the argument between Peter and Susan concerning the size of the telephone bill stands another, more important, issue: how do they deal with the question of responsibility within their growing relationship? It really would not change very much within that particular relationship if a helper of some kind should wave a magic wand over Susan to make her stop using the telephone so often! In other words, people often want solutions to their painful (relational) symptoms, without wanting to undergo a more painful analysis of the underlying causes.

Many are found seeking professional guidance over problems arising out of sterile relationships, while at the same time they resist fiercely any change in their behaviour patterns which are contributing to their problems. And so, as Sheldon Kopp rightly perceives, 'it is not surprising that, though the patient enters therapy insisting that he wants to change, more often than not what he really wants is to remain the same and to get the therapist to make him feel better'.[30] As the word 'patient' suggests, Sheldon Kopp is writing about those undergoing psychotherapy and not marriage counselling, but I doubt if there is a marriage guidance counsellor who has not been asked to 'square the circle' by one or other of the partners in a marriage.

To attempt to remove the symptoms (that is, to make life more comfortable and easy) while ignoring the underlying causes of those symptoms simply makes matters worse. It would mean that, for instance, Peter would have to hold his tongue about Susan's irresponsible behaviour, to deny his right to the free expression of his feelings, and to play the marital game of 'Let's pretend'. More importantly, perhaps, Susan would be ignorant of his real feelings, so she could go on happily believing that he approved of her extravagant whims.

Or take Paula and Steve (chapter 3). It would be natural (if mistaken) to place all the blame on to Steve for his affair with Brenda. However, when counselling couples it is always the *relationship* (that is, the dynamics concerning the way they *relate*) that is the prime focus, not just the particular behaviour by one

of the partners. Beneath the 'problem' of Steve's affair lay the
deeper issue: how could both Paula *and* Steve be helped to uncover
their feelings about each other in an open and honest manner?
Steve could well have been blamed by Paula, and put in the doghouse for a while; he could even have eaten humble pie and 'been
a good boy' at the office. But this would have left untouched the
underlying disease which contributed significantly to the affair in
the first place, hence it would be quite likely to reoccur. Paula
and Steve had a style of communicating which involved endless
questions and a search for *information*, rather than one in which
they both felt free to express their *feelings*. Through the affair with
Brenda, both Paula and Steve created a space within which to
begin listening to one another.

Something rather similar happened to Mike and Brenda
through the affair with Steve. They needed to learn how to *risk*
sharing their inner feelings and needs, rather than concealing
them through the process of protection. Michael Scott Peck, in
his most illuminating book, *The Road Less Travelled* writes:

> Since true listening is love in action, nowhere is it more
> appropriate than in marriage. Yet most couples never truly
> listen to each other. Consequently, when couples come to
> us for counselling or therapy, a major task we must
> accomplish if the process is to be successful is to teach
> them how to listen.[31]

Mike and Brenda illustrated how differently the outcome is to the
style which Paula and Steve started out with. By listening to one
another instead of hurling accusations and counter-accusations at
one another, they could enter into each other's world of feelings
and appreciate thereby each other's needs, hopes and fears. This
always involves the process of risk-taking.

As I write these words, a couple are on their way home after
seeing me for a counselling session. They could be Mike and
Brenda or Paula and Steve. They are back together again after a
short time during which the husband has been staying with another
woman. Both highly intelligent and articulate people, somehow
they never found a model for applying their communication skills
within their marriage. They played 'guessing-games' ('I thought
he would know how I feel!'). Although both deeply hurt by the
experience, they are in the painful process which Mike, Brenda,
Paula and Steve found themselves in: mending their fences and

trying to break new ground on which to build a more satisfying relationship. I said previously (p. 68) that an affair does not *automatically* mean the end of a relationship; this evening I re-experienced the truth of these words in the lives of two people who are taking the risk of trusting one another again, and of applying some of the Guidelines to their newly emerging relationship.

I mentioned (p. 8) that the principles which lie behind these Guidelines have a wider application across the field of human relationships. I have focused them upon 'couples' and taken my illustrations from heterosexual relationships. However, it is my belief that these Guidelines are, in essence, human skills rather than purely skills available only to men and women who are trying to share their lives together. Even within that narrow context I am bound to be accused of being a starry-eyed optimist by some of my readers. I can only give my experience to support my belief in their true effectiveness in the lives of the many couples whom it has been my privilege to help. True, some have found in the process of counselling that there are irreconcilable differences between them which have led to the decision to separate. At least they have done so better equipped to deal with the leave-taking process and to take with them a new style of relating based on integrity and truth.

For other couples, their issues will revolve around those we noticed operating between Molly and Brian. These were characterised by what I call the 'sacrifice syndrome', whereby Molly was making all the concessions in order not to disturb Brian's inferiority complex. In order for him not to feel too threatened by Molly's career she chose to sacrifice her due advancement, in fulfilment of her own potential, upon the altar of Brian's ego. In order to change this pattern, Molly had to risk confronting Brian's negativity and any subsequent hostility. I know this is a risk many partners are unwilling to take, but they must face the consequences of their actions: they cannot play the blaming game ('If it weren't for you . . .') while at the same avoiding the confrontation which could help the 'weaker' partner to deal with the hidden agenda beneath the weakness. There is much misery among many of the marriages which I hear about simply because of this 'mask of false humility'. The partner who chooses to play this particular game may well find that they bear a grudge in spite of (or because of) their 'sacrifice' to the relationship which will come out in hidden ways, like poison seeping into the soul of their life together.

The issue of helplessness we noticed operating between Roger and Jane illustrated the way in which a pattern of behaviour might, at an early stage of their relationship, have worked well ('Me-mother – you-little-boy'!), while at another stage of their relationship it would start to drive one partner round the bend. Jane finally decided to give up mothering Roger, who put up a good fight to retain the *status quo*; but when one partner changes the script they have lived by, there is no *status quo*. Some couples find this change taking place when a real baby is born, and the natural mothering instinct is withdrawn from the husband and rightly diverted to the child. This is often a time of crisis for the family because their old script is changing and the husband will usually feel left out of his wife's affection. Such feelings need ventilating and the adjustments made in order to satisfy the legitimate needs of mother, father and baby. It affords the relationship an opportunity for a 'course correction' into a more mature way of handling the way they relate.

The argument between John and Pat illustrated the need for honest feelings to be expressed in place of the suppression of those feelings under the guise of protection. John needed to find a new way to deal with Pat's passive aggression and he found it in honest confrontation and by the ability of speaking the truth in love. His style of arguing was in the form of caring confrontation, or what David Augsburger calls 'care-fronting'. He found a means of bridge-building from where he was to where Pat was. To go on protecting Pat from his deepest feelings was a means of avoidance which only served to reinforce Pat's silences. Since her silences were paying-off, she had no motivation to change. Couples who continue to collude with their partners' destructive behaviour patterns have only themselves to blame for the outcome.

Sooner or later, in any ongoing relationship, the question is going to arise, 'Who's in charge?' This was amply demonstrated in the dialogue between Simon and Karen (chapter 8). It raises the thorny issue of power and dominance and the need to control the other person. By playing upon Simon's apparent incompetence, Karen was reinforcing his helplessness and by a process of systematic devaluation was eating away at the heart of Simon's self-esteem. They needed to find a new way of building up each other, rather than tearing one another down. At its worst, it becomes the vicious and merciless onslaught of a George and Martha (see p. 34–5) wherein no quarter is asked or given; it is a fight involving 'total war'. But at least George and Martha knew what they were doing – they had almost become addicted to that way of relating. Simon's only awareness would have been his deep feelings of resentment if ever he allowed them to rise within him. Couples who play the 'power game' are often, however, concealing their own innate weaknesses. Lacking *self*-control, they set out to control others.

Issues of control can centre around the question of money, or the way decisions are made or tasks allocated. To see this at its most hilarious yet tragically pathetic extent, we have only to recall the TV series, *Ever Decreasing Circles* (BBC1). The anti-hero, Martin, always adjusts the telephone receiver on entering his house so that it is the 'right' way round; his house is so ordered that it resembles more a military establishment than a home. His form of control, of course, drives his long-suffering wife to distraction. In other households, however, the 'Martin syndrome' is no laughing matter. (Even Maria in *The Sound of Music* did not find it so among the Von Trapp family!)

Power can be demonstrated either in subtle or in more blatant form. The fear of reprisals if the dominant partner is crossed operates in more marriages than we care to admit. It gives birth to the 'I-daren't!' syndrome, and in order to discover how power is operating in your relationships you have only to ask yourself, 'What is it I dare not tell my partner?' Then that is the way you give away your power, by allowing them to take away your right to free expression. It is not so much a question of anyone being more powerful than another; it is rather that, by busily giving away your power, the other person merely appears more powerful, since now they have their own share, plus yours! No wonder you feel powerless and vulnerable.

I recall vividly an experience in the context of my own personal therapy which proved to be of crucial importance in my life. I had reached the 'I-daren't!' syndrome regarding an important relationship I was discussing with my therapist. Invited to confront the person concerned, I lamely replied, 'Oh, I daren't do that!' thinking that would be an end to the matter. To my astonishment, my therapist suddenly got furious with me and I recoiled from her blistering statement, 'The power you're giving to that bloody woman!' As I struggled to understand the import of her accusation I discovered how I had been colluding in a power game. Those words came to me like the voice of God from Mount Sinai, dissolving the scales from my eyes, and I saw clearly for the first time what I had been doing in that particular relationship. I had been giving my power away – and my therapist let me know it in no uncertain terms. This proved to be a turning-point in my life, with very painful results, but at least I found my own integrity again in the process.

Part of the wider application of these principles of human relation skills would obviously concern the whole of a family. There are in fact families which live by the application of some such Guidelines as I have suggested. There can be direct means of self-expression in place of the often sneaky and indirect ways some people adopt. People in families can start to live by a pattern of behaviour which includes the owning and expression of emotions deeply felt. There are families in which there is at least as much listening as talking, where arguments stand on their own merits without dragging in the opinions or undigested prejudices of other people, and where needs are conveyed openly and clearly to one another. In some families the members are capable of not taking responsibility for anyone else's feelings but their own, but in a deep and caring way and with respect for the other person. It is just that most of us have never witnessed such families.

I recall an incident during my studies in Chicago which made me believe in this possibility. I was in a huge station wagon, travelling north from Chicago to Rockford with Ray, a fellow student, his wife and two sons who were in sleeping bags in the back. During our conversation one of the boys whined, 'Mommy, tell Eric to stop kicking me.' I was all ears to know how 'mommy' would deal with this situation. Birgitta simply said, 'What would you like to tell Eric about that?' to which the lad replied, 'Eric, stop kicking me; it hurts.' The response was an immediate apology, and we never heard another sound from either of them until we reached our destination. I had never heard such an adult reply from a parent before. Her son was wanting mommy to fight his battles for him, when of course he was perfectly able to do so himself. Mommy did not rescue him, but reminded him of his own inner resources to confront Eric directly. Having done so, mommy did not have to act as 'piggy-in-the-middle' and appear as the enemy of Eric. Birgitta was inviting her son to take responsibility for what he was allowing Eric to do to him.

What of the world of politics? Could these Guidelines have any effect on our national and international life? Some of them would surely have a profound effect in enabling discussions to break out of the endless round of accusations and counter-accusations, of suspicion and projection and wilful misrepresentation. I would invite those of you who would appreciate hearing how it might sound for the leaders of, say, the USA and the USSR to communicate using some of these relational insights to read the imaginative dialogue by William Schutz in his *Here Comes Everybody*.[32] Even with this couple of VIPs, there can be a new and positive approach to international communications.

Industry, too, has often been a graveyard of attempts at conciliatory communication. Much of it has been marked by the 'sound and fury' model, signifying nothing. Some of these attempts are marked by the senseless use of depersonalising labels, generalisations and stereotyping the opposition. Where the Guidelines are applicable to the impersonal world of industrial relations, rather than the personal world of intimate relationships, substantial allowances would have to be made. Like all good à-la-carte menus, the customers are invited to choose what most suits their palate.

Finally, in education there seems to me to be a crying need for the teaching of human relationship skills to be taken seriously. There are principles of self-expression which could quite easily be placed in the school syllabus, certainly as young as the Junior School age. Role-plays and videos depicting real-life situations which contain positive ways of expressing ourselves to other people would be in strong contrast to the often violent and negative dialogues which pour from our TV screens and which have such a deleterious effect on our children. It is not good enough to lament the poor quality of television 'families' and the way our children are affected thereby. We need an alternative model to place before our children, not just condemnation. Where better to find this alternative model than in families where the parents themselves are living examples of open and honest communication and where such fighting as exists is for the relationship and the general good of the whole family? Teaching our children at school to argue constructively, therefore, could be a valuable adjunct to its reinforcement in their homes. Such an idea has not been tried and found wanting; it has not (to my knowledge) been tried.

One of the difficulties I have encountered in writing this book has been keeping to the strict boundaries I set myself not to stray far (if at all) into the realm of psychotherapy. To the professional counsellors who form part of my readership I wish to add a few comments.

First, I have had in mind non-professional readers and, however it has turned out, at least my aim has been to keep this book as non-technical as I could. It was out of my own need for some such handbook which I could recommend to the couples who come to see me about their personal relationships that it came to birth in the first place.

Second, one early critic of my work reminded me (I was, as it turned out, quite aware of the fact) that in the case of George and Martha in *Who's Afraid of Virginia Woolf?* (see pp. 34–5) their need to 'fight dirty' is probably linked to unconscious (irrational) factors which in turn ensured they kept their distance from each other. Of course, I would not disagree with that. Some relationships founder because of a far deeper malaise than even the issues I have uncovered beneath the relational symptoms. It has been tempting to start 'peeling the onion' of individual personalities down to the origins of character disorders and neuroses but I have had to resist that path. In a further book, I hope to be able to pay attention to this important area and to show some of the ways in which our personalities can be damaged and a practical way in which they might be healed. But in *Couples Arguing* I have kept to the narrower field of uncovering some of the conscious (rather than the unconscious) factors which destroy harmony between couples and how they can be improved in the 'here-and-now'. The 'there-and-then' issues must await another day.

Notes

1. Genesis 3.13, RSV.

2. *Hutchinson 20th Century Encyclopedia*, ed. E. M. Horsley (4th edn, 1981), p. 420.

3. *Marriage, Faith and Love*, Jack Dominian (Darton, Longman & Todd, 1981), p. 213.

4. ibid.

5. Originally transmitted in 1986 on Channel 4.

6. In my view, the dialogues between Mary Beth and Harvey Lacey are usually good examples of an adult arguing style and illustrate many of these Guidelines.

7. For a fuller treatment on how protection works in a relationship, see the dialogue and analysis between John and Pat in chapter 7.

8. An excellent introduction to this subject will be found in the highly readable *Families, and How to Survive Them* by Robin Skynner and John Cleese, Methuen, 1983.

9. Compare Roger and Jane in chapter 6.

10. *Marriage, Faith and Love* (see note 3), p. 125.

11. *Yes, Minister*, vol. III, ed. Johnathan Lynn and Antony Jay (BBC Publications, 1983), p. 173f.

12. For a helpful outline on the different levels of human communication, see *Why Am I Afraid to Tell You Who I Am?*, John Powell (Fontana/Collins, 1969), pp. 50–62.

13. *Creative Process in Gestalt Therapy*, Joseph Zinker (Vintage Books, 1978), p. 213.

14. cf. Sir Humphrey Appleby's statement on p. 13.

15. cf. the quotation from Jack Dominian on p. 2.

16. *Open Marriage*, Nena and George O'Neill (Avon, 1972), p. 126.

17. *Games People Play*, Eric Berne (Penguin, 1975), pp. 96ff.

18. *Who's Afraid of Virginia Woolf?* Edward Albee (Cape, 1964). Quoted by courtesy of the author.

19. *The Intimate Enemy*, George R. Bach and Peter Wyden, Avon, 1970.

20. *The Growing Edge of Gestalt Therapy*, ed. Edward W. L. Smith (Brunner/Mazel, 1976), p. 15.

21. *Clinical Theology*, Frank Lake (Darton, Longman and Todd, 1966), p. 1014.

22. *David Copperfield*, Charles Dickens (Heron Books, 1967), vol. I, p. 280.

23. ibid., vol. II, p. 376f.

24. *Caring Enough to Confront*, David Augsburger, Marshall Pickering, 1985.

25. *Beginnings without End*, Sam Keen (Harper & Row, 1975), p. 8.

26. For example, M. E. P. Seligman in *Helplessness*, Freeman, 1975.

27. Compare John on p. 104.

28. *Beginnings without End* (see note 25), p. 130.

29. *If You Meet the Buddha on the Road, Kill Him!* Sheldon Kopp (Sheldon Press, 1974), p. 3 (my italics).

30. ibid., p. 2.

31. *The Road Less Travelled*, Michael Scott Peck (Simon & Schuster, 1978), p. 128.

32. *Here Comes Everybody*, William C. Schutz (Harper & Row, 1971), pp. 266–73.

Suggestions for Further Reading

FOR THE ORDINARY READER:

I'm OK – You're OK, Thomas A. Harris, Pan Books, 1970.
Families and How to Survive Them, Robin Skynner and John Cleese, Methuen, 1983.
Caring Enough to Confront, David Augsburger, Marshall Pickering, 1985.
Born to Win, Muriel James and Dorothy Jongeward, Addison-Wesley Publishing Co., 1976.
Women Who Love Too Much, Robin Norwood, Arrow Books, 1986.
Why Can't Men Open Up? Steven Naifeh and Gregory White Smith, Sphere Books, 1987.

FOR THE PROFESSIONAL COUNSELLOR:

One Flesh: Separate Persons, A. C. Robin Skynner, Constable, 1976 (contains the principles of marital and family psychotherapy).
Peoplemaking, Virginia Satir, Souvenir Press, 1972 (a classic by a leading family therapist).
Make or Break, Jack Dominian, SPCK, 1986 (an introduction to marriage counselling).
The Intimate Enemy, George R. Bach and Peter Wyden, Avon, 1968 (a wordy, American publication with the theme of creative aggression; now out of print).
Open Marriage, Nena and George O'Neill, Avon, 1972 (subtitled 'A New Life Style for Couples').
The Initmate Marriage, Howard and Charlotte Clinebell, Harper & Row, 1970.
The New Male–Female Relationship, Herb Goldberg, Coventure, 1983 (deals with issues of sexism and on finding new roles).

Counselling Agencies

Among the professional agencies who specialise in couples counselling are:

The National Marriage Guidance Council
Head Office:
    Herbert Gray College,
    Little Church Street,
    RUGBY,
    Warwickshire CV21 3AP (tel. 0788–73241)
or see in your local telephone directory under 'Marriage Guidance Council'.

The Catholic Marriage Advisory Council
    15 Lansdowne Road,
    Holland Park,
    LONDON W11 3AJ (tel. 01–727 0141)
or see in your local telephone directory

The British Association for Counselling
    37A Sheep Street,
    RUGBY,
    Warwickshire CV21 3BX (tel. 0788–78328/9)
The BAC produce an up-to-date directory of counsellors in various parts of the country, most of whom offer marital counselling.

Index